# *Practical Samāyā Tantra*

# *Practical Samāyā Tantra*

Dale M. Buegel, M.D. E-RYT 500

Published by
Vitality Matters, LLC

ISBN 978-1-54393-172-3
Vitality Matters, LLC
1600 W. Green Tree Road, #312
Glendale, WI, 53209
U.S.A.

I dedicate this book to my teacher and the lineage of teachers whom he served. My teacher consciously left his body in November, 1996. He was known in the West as Swami Rama of the Himalayas. In India he was known by various names, Bhole Baba, Bhole Prabu, Dandi Swami Sadashiva Bharati, to name a few. Some claim that in older times he was known as Swami Rama Tirtha, or in more ancient times by a Biblical name.

I asked Swami Rama to be taught in silence. I wanted to actually experience what is written about in ancient texts. I did not wish to simply read the texts or hear lectures about them. Swami Rama and those guides that continue to work with him have been very generous in facilitating my growth on the path of yoga, and for that I am grateful.

"Guru is not a person. It is a force driven by grace."

Swami Rama

# Contents

## *Preface*

The path of samāyā tantra is sometimes called the quiet path, the right-hand path, or the internal path of tantra. Many of its practices contained in this text make use of the perceptions of the subtle senses. It is the subtle senses that allow one to explore the flows and rhythms of the prāṇas that invite the guides and open the gateways to the subtle self.

The perspective of this author is that of a practitioner, not a scholar. My teacher encouraged me to practice and learn to perceive the flows and rhythms of the prāṇas. This direct perception is called prāṇa dhāraṇā, focus on the prāṇas.

For many years I resisted teaching many of the subtle practices revealed to me. I had been warned by those in the traditions of yoga that too much dissemination of knowledge could be dangerous for the world. As I live my life it appears the world is quite capable of unbalancing itself through ignorance. Perhaps it is time for some of humanity to understand the subtleties of self, the subtleties of the process of life and death, and to consciously experience the connection of the individual self with the whole. As I begin the work of writing this text, I hope that what is revealed in this text may be helpful to some who, like me, have wished to explore the limits of human potential and have wished to understand the union of self to the whole.

Dale M. Buegel, August 19th$^{th}$, 2016

## *Acknowledgements*

I give thanks to my teacher, Swami Rama, who always said I should write more.

I also give thanks to Swami Veda Bharati who introduced me to the teachings of yoga and who also introduced me to Swami Rama more than four decades ago. I also thank Pandit Rajmani Tigunait who, in addition to Swami Veda, helped with the teaching of some specific practices over the years of my training. I also thank the unmanifest guides that open the gateways of knowledge when the time is correct to do so. I thank Dr. John Upledger for introducing me to the subtleties of manual medicine, specifically craniosacral motion, myofascial rhythms, and their energetic components.

In addition, I thank my students for continually challenging me to find ways to present the subject of yoga in a practical format. I also thank Michaela Feriancikova for allowing me to use photographs of her to illustrate some specific practices. For the use of photographic expertise and equipment and for blessed inspiration, I also thank Ragani Buegel. I also thank Ragani for posing for three photographs.

## The Path of Samāyā Tantra

As one contemplates the goal of the different practices contained in this text, it is important to understand the definition of samāyā tantra. The definition my teacher gave of samāyā was "I am with You". "You" in this context means Śakti, the feminine aspect of the Divine, the force of creation. "Sa" in this context is translated as "with". This does not mean walking down the street with or being in the same room with. "With" means being merged with, having become one with. There is then no separation in awareness or consciousness between oneself and Śakti. (For help with Sanskrit pronunciation, please see the pronunciation guide preceding the glossary section of this text).

"Māyā" in the context of samāyā tantra is the entirety of the organization of energies and vibrations that we call the manifest universe. All the textures of the elements that are mixed and organized into what we term "matter" are aspects of māyā. Also part of māyā is the force of the Divine that organizes those textures of the elements. The element ākāśa (ether or space) interacts with Śakti to modify the infinite energy potential contained within the silence of ākāśa to manifest as an organization of the textures of earth, water, fire, and air within a particular space. All the objects of the world including a brick, a morsel of food, our bodies, and everything that we experience as part of the manifest universe is a product of the union of Śakti with ākāśa.

"Tantra" is sometimes defined as a body of spiritual knowledge or defined as a particular tradition of spiritual science. The word “tantra” is thought to be derived from its root words “tanoti” (expands, accomplish, extend toward, direct toward) and the word “tra” (tools or instrument for accomplishing a purpose).

“Tantra” in the context of samāyā tantra means to take that which is out of balance, of untruth, evil, ugly, and transmute or transform it into that which is in balance, of truth, good, and beautiful through the application of the power of overwhelming love and compassion (Śakti). This definition of tantra comes from the journal of a master of left hand tantra read to me nearly twenty years ago in the courtyard of Krim-Kund ashram in Varanasi.

***Something to consider:***

Are you content to have your mind drive your consciousness? Would you prefer instead to have the mind be a tool of consiousness?

Should you decide to direct your life toward the latter choice, please consider the following: In this text we will explore the interface of the path of samāyā tantra and its practices with the eight limbs of yoga. Sincerity of effort in achieving balance of energies and balance of life attract the grace that illuminates the continuation of the path. Attachment to the results of one’s practice can take one on a detour from the path into areas of darkness where the illumination of grace no longer shines.

# The Nature of Cakras

Cakras are described and depicted many different ways by various authors and honored traditions. When portrayed artistically there may be common elements, but colors, shapes, and other characteristics often vary. If we wish to truly understand the cakras, we must learn to experience them directly. The practices in this book were chosen to help gather experience at each of the major cakras.

Where the channels through which prāṇa flows (nādīs) intersect, an energetic entity called a cakra can be found. The components of a cakra are as follows:

1. Primary anatomical correlations related to each cakra: For example, the liver and stomach each have a relationship with maṇipūra cakra.

2. Primary energetic relationships, such as the energetic orbits of the eyes depicted as two lotus petals in representations of ājñā cakra.

3. Cakras have radiance, rhythms and flows of prāṇa associated with each cakra. These energetic subtleties will be discussed in later chapters.

4. When the energetic rhythms and flows of prāṇa are balanced, the bindus (null points or gateways) of each cakra provide the opening for the force driven by grace, called "guru", to illuminate one's consciousness. As my teacher said, because cakras can embody consciousness, they have the ability to teach a practitioner.

The role of practices described in the following chapters on the cakras is to provide the tools to balance the flows and rhythms of prāṇa at each major cakra. As these rhythms and flows balance, the invitation to attend to the central energy of suṣumnā awareness leads to the opening of the bindus, those seeds of energy potential that are part of each cakra. Familiarizing oneself with each individual cakra will help facilitate mastery of practices involving more than one cakra.

# Rhythms and Flows of Prāṇa

The breath is often described as the vehicle for prāṇa. While some of the major flows of prāṇa are related to breathing, there are flows and rhythms of prāṇa that are not timed with physical respiration.

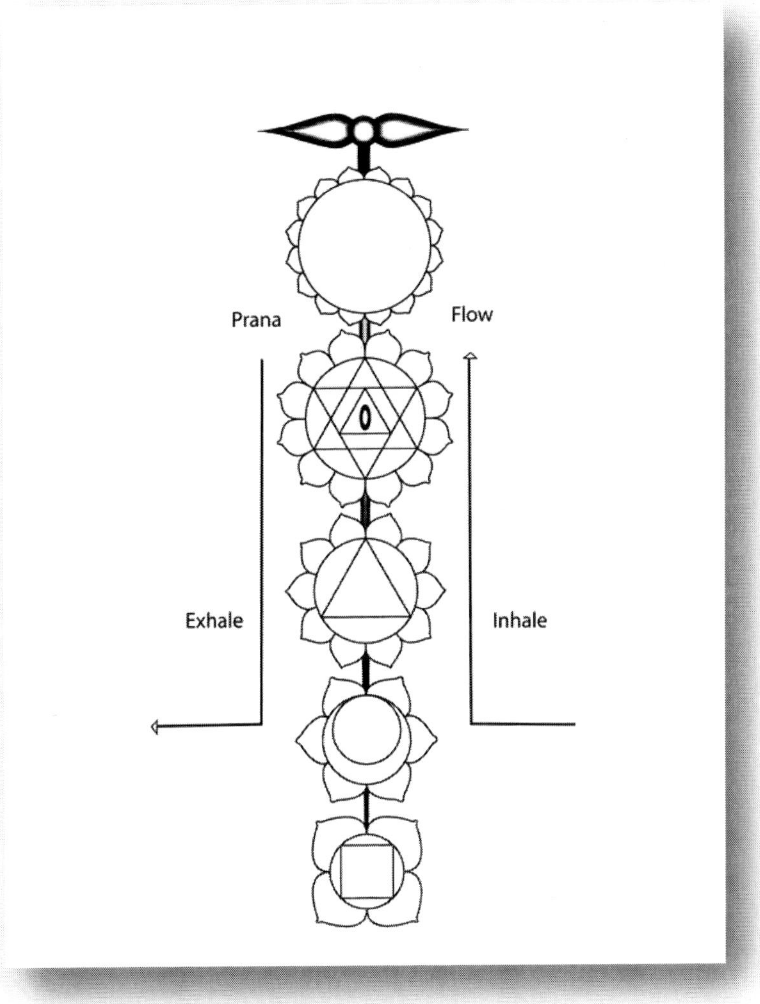

The foregoing illustration shows the flow of prāṇa that accompanies breathing. During exhalation prāṇa flows down the central channel and also flows out laterally from each and every cakra in every direction from the central area of each cakra. During inhalation prāṇa flows from every direction toward the center of each cakra and joins the upward flow of the central channel.

The central channel of flow is generally referred to as suṣumṇa. The external aspect of this central channel supports the flow of prāṇa that accompanies breathing. The more internal aspect of suṣumṇa is reserved for the energy of Śakti.

One rhythm of prāṇa that does not depend or correlate with respiration is the dance between the "ha" and "tha". My teacher defined "hatha yoga" as the union of the right energy ("ha", piṅgalā) and left energy ("tha", iḍā). Hatha yoga practices, both āsana and prāṇāyāma, support bringing into union the right and the left energies. The result of this union is the application of suṣumṇa awareness. When the dance between the "ha" and "tha" is perfectly balanced and/or comes to stillness, the gateways to experiencing aspects of the subtle body and ultimately to experiencing the reality of Oneself are opened.

Another rhythm of prāṇa that does not depend or correlate with respiration involving activity of the lungs and diaphragm is the energetic component of what osteopathic physicians call myofascial rhythm or craniosacral rhythm. Craniosacral rhythm is also sometimes called cranio-respiratory rhythm. The driving force for this rhythm is fluctuating pressure of cerebrospinal fluid in the central nervous system. Anatomy is designed to accommodate fluctuating pressures with movement of skull sutures and flexibility of the dura, the membrane that encapsulates the central nervous system and cerebrospinal fluid. Because of the attachments of the dura to the fourth cervical vertebra and to the sacrum, subtle movement of fascia throughout the body can be experienced as a myofascial rhythm. Craniosacral and myofascial rhythms can be felt as physical movement. Dr. John Upledger taught me in 1983 that these physiological rhythms also have an energetic component which can be perceived with one's tactile senses. The rhythms of fluctuating pressure in the central nervous system and myofascial rhythm are independent of pulmonary respiration.

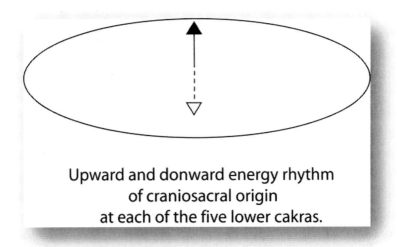

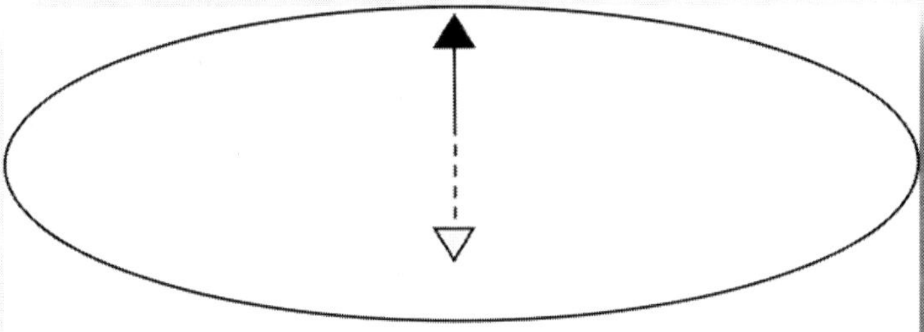

Upward and donward energy rhythm of craniosacral origin at each of the five lower cakras.

In the image above, the subtle upward and downward rhythmic flow of prāṇa occurs in the area of suṣumṇa at the central area of each cakra. Breath does not affect this rhythm.

## Pratyāhāra

Pratyāhāra is that limb of yoga where the mind learns to no longer attend to one's gross senses. As my teacher pointed out, suspending gross sensory perception (ordinary touch, sight, hearing, taste, and smell) while preserving the subtle senses is helpful for monitoring the rhythms and flows of prāṇa. In particular, Swami Rama recommended for me to preserve the subtle sense of touch. Those tactile sensations of the prāṇa flows and rhythms can be very helpful when one is trying to balance the "ha" and "tha" or is trying to discover the gateway within a cakra.

In the following chapter are a set of practices that are helpful for establishing awareness of the subtleties of yoga practice. While focusing on subtle sensations, it is helpful to have an environment that is relatively free of gross sensory distractions. Soft light or darkness, relative quiet, and a comfortable temperature are all helpful when first learning these practices.

Later one can learn to attend to subtle sensations while engaged in everyday activities. Be practical, however. Attending to subtle sensations while driving, for example, can be quite hazardous. I recall Swami Veda Bharati telling of his experience of having run a red light while trying to practice the subtleties of alternate nostril breathing.

# Building Awareness of the Subtle

The purpose of this chapter is to allow the practitioner to develop the tools necessary to experience the radiance, rhythms, and flows of the subtle energy system.

## *Diaphragmatic Breathing*

One of the challenges facing the practitioner during transitions in consciousness is to maintain steadiness of focus. The practice of diaphragmatic breathing allows one to develop that serene steadiness of focus during transitions in the breath. In the beginning the mind will take every opportunity to divert the practitioner's focus. Transitions between phases of the breath and transitions between the different sounds of a mantra used during the practice of diaphragmatic breathing each allow the practitioner to master remaining steady during transitions. In the yoga traditions the mantra "soḥaṃ" is merged with the breath in a particular pattern. The sound of this mantra "sssss", "ooo", "ḥ ḥ ḥ", "ā ā ā", "ṃ ṃ ṃ", is created in the mind in such a way that each sound is merged into the next sound. There are no breaks in the repetition of the mantra, including between the "ṃ" and "s" sounds.

**1.** Assume a position with an erect spine, either seated or supine.

**2.** Relax the body, particularly relaxing the intercostal muscles between the ribs.

**3.** Gently contract the diaphragm muscle during inhalation, allowing the diaphragm to press downward against the abdominal contents. This will expand the belly. Find the endpoint of the diaphragm's contraction which will fully expand the belly and flare out the lower ribs. Full diaphragmatic contraction allows for a smooth transition between inhalation and exhalation. Some individuals may have weakness in the midline of their abdomen because of certain medical conditions and may have to limit the contraction of the diaphragm to less than full expansion of the belly.

**4.** Following an inhalation, smoothly transition to exhalation, drawing the navel gently toward the spine. Just before exhalation ends, once again begin a gentle transition by contracting the diaphragm. Once the practitioner has developed perception of prāṇa, there is a subtle energetic wave that develops between the navel and the pelvic floor as exhalation merges into inhalation. Sensing the subtle transitions of that energetic wave helps to smooth transitions between phases of the breath.

**5.** Any irregularity or pause in the breath will allow the mind to change its focus. For this reason, the practitioner asks the mind to focus on a particular mantra that can be easily combined with the breath. The mantra "soḥaṃ" merges easily with the flow of the breath, "sssooo" being used with the inhalation, and "ḥḥḥaaaṃṃṃ" being used with the exhalation. Remember to smooth the transitions "oooḥḥḥ" and "ṃṃṃsss" that occur during transitions between phases of the breath. Doing so will help prevent any hesitation or pause between phases of the breath.

**6.** To deepen this practice, the practitioner can allow the vibration of the sounds of the mantra to resonate at a particular point of focus. The navel is a useful point to use for this purpose. As one gains experience with this practice and begins to feel the energetic flow, one can sense the energy moving inward through the navel during inhalation and outward through the navel during exhalation. The vibration of the mantra can start to merge with these flows. It is helpful to define a particular point in the exact center of the navel where the mind can remain fixed and develop its awareness of subtleties. It is also helpful to silently intone the vibration of the mantra used at the point of focus.

### *Nostril Awareness*

Focusing on sensations in the nostrils while breathing is one way to build subtle tactile sensitivity. During everyday life, one nostril is always somewhat more dominant than the other. For most people, a shift in dominance tends to occur every one to three hours. Anatomical restrictions such as a deviated septum may interfere with this natural rhythm. Training the nostrils to approximate equal airflow in each nostril can improve the practitioner's focus during meditation practice. Equalizing flow is one tool to bring the energies of the "ha" and "tha" to union, or balance.

**1.** Establish diaphragmatic breathing at a sufficient rate that the flow of breath in the nostrils can be felt. Coolness on the inhale and the warmth on the exhale should be apparent. This practice can be done in a seated or supine position.

**2.** Determine which nostril is active, has the most airflow. If you cannot distinguish which nostril has more air flow, simply pick one nostril upon which you wish to focus.

**3.** During inhalation feel the coolness in that nostril, and during exhalation feel the warmth. Narrow the focus in order to define the point in the nostril that feels the absolute coolest during inhalation. Stay focused at that single point, feeling the coolness during inhalation and the warmth during exhalation at that single point. To intensify the focus, try to determine the exact moments of transition between the sensations of coolness and the sensations of warmth.

**4.** Switch focus to the opposite nostril and repeat step three in that nostril.

**5.** Now focus on both points simultaneously, one point in each nostril. Try to have the intensity of focus be exactly the same in each nostril. The mind will tend to focus on one point more than the other or to shift focus from point-to-point. For this step try to maintain exactly equal focus on each point. The response of the nostrils to this step is to become more equal in flow. This produces an energetic effect of tending to bring the right and the left energies, the "ha" and "tha" closer to union, or balance. A sign that this balance is occurring is that the practitioner's awareness receives an invitation to attend to the space between the air flows. This invitation is a result of the force of grace being drawn to the preparation of the energies. Such preparation and grace may result in the activation of suṣumṇa awareness, an awareness of the central channel.

Pictured at the top of the following diagram is ājñā cakra with its two lotus petals. Spiraling around the central energy channel, suṣumṇā, are the left and right nādīs of iḍā and piṅgalā. It is a diagram representing the human energy system of nādīs and cakras. The left and right spiraling energies are often depicted as snakes. This is because the nādīs of iḍā and piṅgalā are constantly dancing with each other.

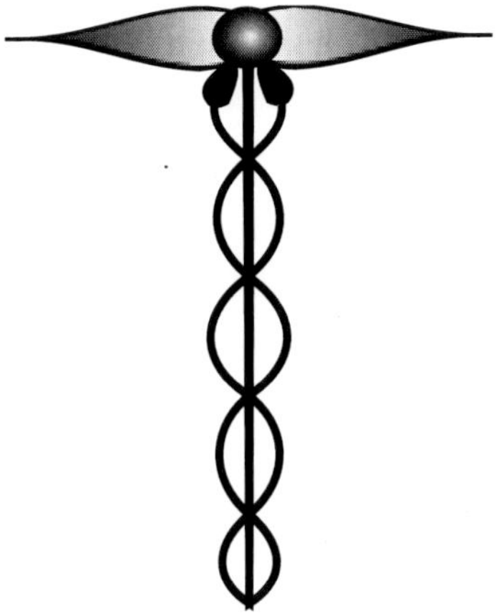

If focus is applied in a way where the dance between iḍā and piṅgalā comes to stillness, or union, the gateway to suṣumṇā becomes available. The central energy of the diagram, usually depicted as a dormant staff or rod, becomes active and allows the practitioner to experience the meditative state called suṣumṇā awareness.

### *Dance Between the "Ha" and the "Tha"*

In the preceding practice of nostril awareness, the practitioner may become aware of the relationship between the points in the nostrils defined by steps three and four in the previous technique. There is a side to side dance between iḍā and piṅgalā that can be felt while studying the relationship between the defined points in the nostrils. My teacher used to describe this dance as being like the eddy of water behind the tail of a large fish as it slowly swims through the water. The energy sweeps gently side to side as iḍā and piṅgalā dance with each other. This dance between the "ha" and the "tha" is independent of the rate at which one breathes.

My teacher described three areas of focus where this dance could more easily be felt.

**1.** Side to side through the nose bridge, using the defined points in the nostrils to begin one's focus. It can be helpful to confine one's awareness to a line between the points in each nostril when trying to study the rhythm of the dance.

**2.** Study the dance at the indentation above the upper lip just below the nose, focusing on the prominences of the upper lip to each side of that indentation.

**3.** If one can tactilely sense the energetic orbits of the eyes, one can look for the sweep of energy that dances between those two energetic aspects of ājñā cakra. If one senses the sweep of energy, try to make the amplitude to the right and to the left exactly equal.

**4.** As in the previous technique, the force of grace may invite the practitioner to attend to developing suṣumṇa awareness. This is sometimes felt as a razor thin plane of energy that exactly divides the right and the left. This plane of energy may be felt at the indentation above the upper lip, at the tip of the nose, through the nose bridge, and up to a gateway on the forehead called trikuti cakra. There may be a visual accompaniment during the developing awareness of this plane of energy.

In the following chapter the relationship between the left and right energy channels will be explored by incorporating subtle sensitivities of nostril dominance during āsana practice.

## Studying "Ha" and "Tha" in Āsana Practice

Āsanas not only benefit and prepare the physical body, but also influence prāṇamāyā kośa, the energetic interface between mind and body.

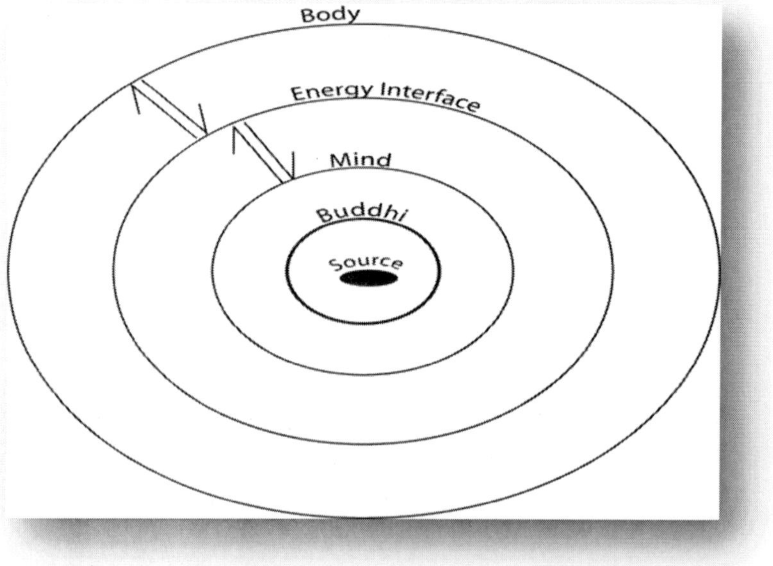


Fascia is the organizational tissue of the body. It organizes muscle fibers into muscles and organizes muscles into groups that can work together. It thickens to form tendons and ligaments. It encapsulates and forms the internal organizational structure of organs such as the liver, kidneys, and spleen. Without fascia organizing the cells of these organs, the organs would not be able to perform their functions. Fascia also thickens to form the dural membrane which helps to protect the central nervous system. Fascia literally interconnects everything in our physical body.

Physiologists tell us that fascia is a liquid crystalline matrix. When particular forces are applied to any crystal a polarity can develop between positive and negative charge. When this occurs in the collagen fibers, elastic fibers, and interspersed liquid that make up our fascia, a bioelectric field influence can be the result of stretching or compressing our fascia during āsana practice. In other words, part of prāṇamāyā kośa is influenced by changes in fascia during our daily yoga practice.

A challenge for the mind is to develop the subtle sensitivities to notice energetic changes during hatha yoga practice. To improve the mind's ability to focus on the subtleties of hatha yoga practice, it is helpful to notice nostril dominance during certain yoga poses. One can also learn to train the shifts in nostril dominance during āsana practice. Doing so helps to facilitate improvement in focus during one's meditation as well.

### *Lower Extremity Lift Nostril Dominance*

While lying on one's side, perform leg raises for both abductors and abductors. Remember to press a lower extremity into the ground with just as much force as it takes to raise the other extremity. This will engage both sets of abductors and help to maintain pelvic symmetry.

While performing these exercises, focus on breath in the nostrils to determine dominance. The nostril closest to the ceiling will try to become more dominant than the nostril closest to the mat.

When one reverses the positions to strengthen the abductors and adductors on the opposite side, the nostrils will switch their dominance. Noticing the subtle shifts of dominance can help train the response of the energetics connected to this dominance. Attending to shifts in nostril dominance during hatha yoga practice can help one learn to adjust breath flow in the nostrils, facilitating the ability to develop suṣumṇa awareness.

*Nostril Dominance During Angle Poses*

Alignment concerns for the following pictured angle poses (lunging with right knee flexed) are as follows:

**1.** Right foot is aligned with the mat.

**2.** Left toes are forward relative to the left heel.

**3.** Left knee is in the plane of the left ankle and left hip. This will minimize the risk of collateral ligament strain.

**4.** Angle of the left knee is not less than 90°. This will minimize the risk of cruciate ligament damage during this pose which has full weight-bearing on the joints.

**5.** The major cakras are in the straight line. This is accomplished by translating the rib cage through engagement of the left paraspinal muscles rather than allowing the rib cage and spine to curve to the right. The central flow through the cakras is unrestricted. For neck support, one draws the chin and head posteriorly, engaging the paraspinal muscles between the upper back and base of the cranium for additional support for the neck.

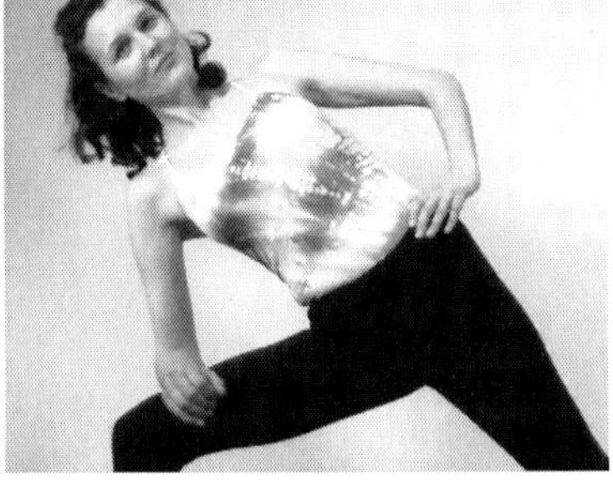

**6.** Keep the left hip support muscles tightly engaged in order to support the hip joint and to not lose support of the muscles in the lower back.

**7.** Pressing both feet into the ground helps to engage the pelvic floor and stabilize the pose.

After initially lining up the pose without head rotation, notice the left nostril's tendency to become dominant. Nostrils can then be balanced by rotating the head to the left until one senses that the right nostril is trying to allow more flow. One is using the neck rotation to partially restrict flow in the left energy channel and open flow in the right energy channel.

One can then perform the pose to the opposite side, noticing the same airflow changes in nostril dominance. Alternatively, one can try to maintain nostril balance while slowly shifting the pose to the opposite side.

Studying nostril dominance in triangle pose is very similar. It can be more difficult for practitioners, however, to maintain alignment of the major cakras while performing trikoṇāsana.

### *Nostril Dominance During Spinal Twists*

It is important to keep the major cakras aligned while performing spinal twists. To help achieve this alignment, practice the following steps.

**1.** Make certain that both ischial tuberosities (sit-bones) are both firmly in contact with the ground regardless of the version of spinal twist being performed.

**2.** Before turning to the right, grasp the right shin to align the spine. Hip flexors and abdominals can hold this alignment while performing step three.

**3.** As one holds the position in step two, begin rotation to the right using the oblique muscles of the abdomen to

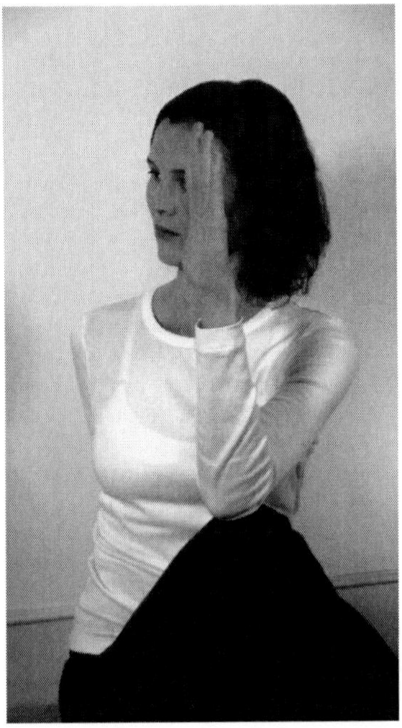

accomplish this. Support for the pose can gently be added when one simultaneously applies downward pressure on the right knee and also applies downward pressure into the ground behind the right hip or sacrum. It is helpful to externally rotate the right shoulder while applying downward pressure behind the torso. This may then allow obtaining support for the torso by pressing the right forearm into the torso. Maintain the alignment of the major cakras if one wishes to study the relative energy flows of the right and left channels while performing the pose.

**4.** Twisting to the right will open the left energy channel and dominance of the left nostril. Most practitioners will need to draw the head posteriorly before rotating the head to keep the major cakras aligned during rotation. The chin should remain parallel to the ground.

Spinal twists can be used to train nostril flow by simply reversing the pose several times. Practicing asymmetric poses such as the spinal twist in this manner will keep the nostril flows closer to equal over time. For those who wish to study the flow of prāṇa during this pose, they may wish to follow the left energy flow downward during exhalation and the central energy upward during inhalation. In the pictured pose, the left flow between ājñā and viśuddha cakra will spiral to the right side between viśuddha cakra and anāhata cakra as well as between maṇipūra cakra and svādiṣṭhāna cakra. When following the flows in this manner, it is helpful to wait for the next segment of the path to appear and invite one's attention before proceeding. This means following the path offered rather than imagining where one thinks the path might be.

Following the spiraling flow of the dominant channel downward and returning upward through the central channel is an example of one prāṇa dhāraṇā practice while performing an āsana. Before one can do such practices, it is helpful to build subtle awareness in order that flows and rhythms of prāṇa can be felt more easily.

### *Seated Poses and Nostril Dominance*

Assume a seated meditation pose where the major cakras are aligned. This means the spine is erect and that the meatus of the ears (openings in the ears), the acromion processes of the shoulders (the knobs on the shoulders), and the greater trochanters (the notch in the thighs below the pelvis when one tightens the gluteus muscles in a standing position) are all in the same plane regardless of the particular pose and supports being used.

**1.** Determine which nostril is the dominant nostril.

**2.** Rotate the head in the direction of the dominant nostril. Hold this position until the dominance begins to shift. When performing this maneuver, make certain the vertex of the skull (crown of the head) rotates without changing its position in space. This will keep the major cakras aligned while the dominance between the nostrils and the left and right energies shifts.

**3.** If one wishes to train the nostrils, simply rotate the head to the opposite side, keeping the major cakras aligned. Repeat the process several times to help the "ha" and "tha" become more responsive to one's focus. With practice, head rotation of only a few degrees may be enough to initiate a shift in nostril dominance.

If one is trying to establish suṣumṇa awareness during meditation, it is helpful to use this method to get the nostrils closer to equal flow before beginning one's meditation practice. Alternatively, one can choose to wait for the nostrils to begin their natural shift on average every 1.5 to 3 hours and attempt to catch the momentary opportunity of exactly equal energetic balance to practice application of suṣumṇa. If one is sufficiently focused, this opportunity may show itself as a tiny speck of light at the exact moment of the shift in nostril dominance.

## Six Major Cakras

In the samāyā tantra tradition, there are practices of prāṇa dhāraṇā associated with each of the major cakras. For some practices, however, the focus of the practitioner is on more than one cakra. Studying the flows and rhythms of each individual cakra is helpful for practices involving more than one cakra.

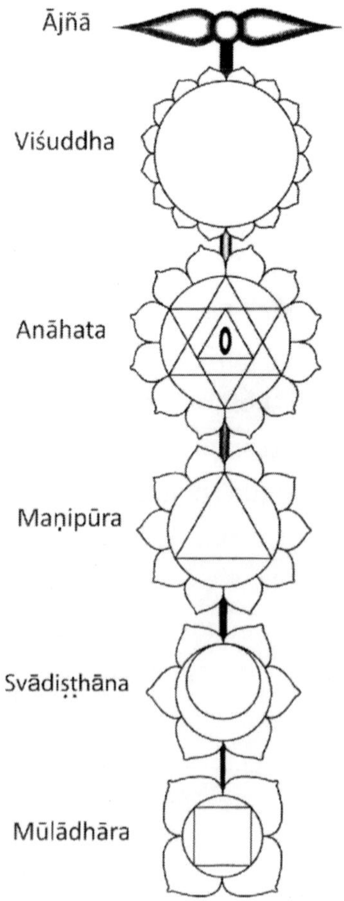

## Ājñā Cakra

There are several methods to balance iḍā and piṅgalā at particular cakras. One method makes use of various trikoṇa, or triangles, to balance the left and right energies. The mantra to be used with these triangles is "aiṃ", pronounced "aaaeeeṃṃṃ". The vibration is drawn out as one traces a triangle or triangles with one's awareness. Some will prefer the sound "ñg" to "ṃ" (a result of not closing the lips when transitioning from "ñg" to "aaa"). "Aiṃ" is the seed mantra of Sarasvatī.

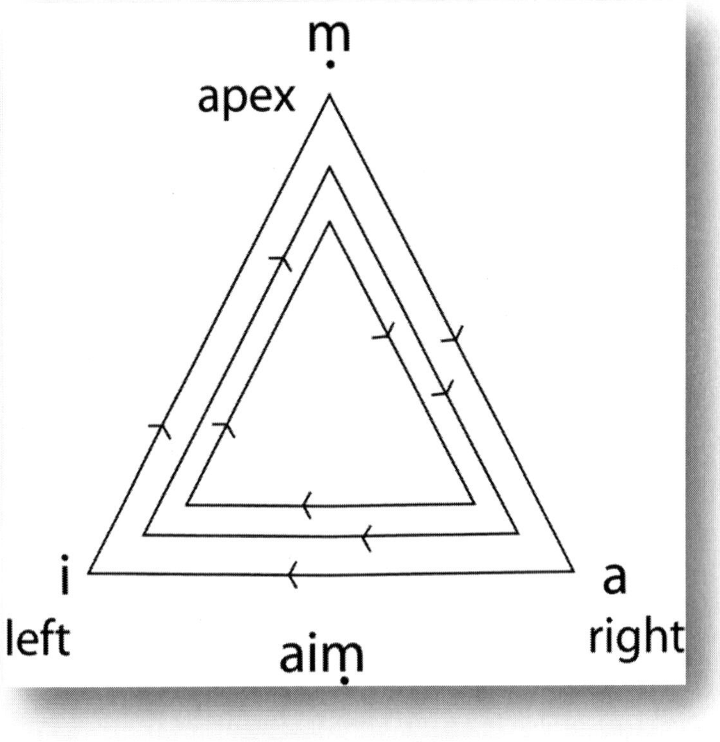


The following is a practice that uses the mantra "aiṃ" with three different triangles. The goal of the practice is to balance the right and left energies of piṅgalā and iḍā in order to establish suṣumṇa awareness.

### *Triangles and Ājñā Cakra*

**1.** Select the points of focus for the particular triangle one wishes to work with.

**2.** One useful triangle is the following:

a. Right point = the point in the right nostril that is the absolute coolest as one inhales.

b. Left point = the point in the left nostril that is the absolute coolest as one inhales.

c. Apex = the gateway of trikuti cakra roughly at the center of the forehead.

**3.** Position oneself with an erect spine that will allow diaphragmatic breathing in either a seated meditation pose or śavāsana.

**4.** Begin by silently intoning the mantra "aaa" at the right point. Make certain the vibration of the mantra merges with the point and is not just a cognitive thought.

**5.** Begin to draw the vibration of the mantra "aaa" toward the point in the left nostril. As one approaches the point in the left nostril, gradually transition the sound of "aaa" to "iii" (pronounced "eee") as one moves the awareness through the left point and upward toward the apex.

**6.** Similarly, as one begins to approach the apex, smoothly transition from "iii" to "ṃṃṃ" or "ñg ñg ñg".

**7.** Smoothly transition from "ṃṃṃ" or "ñg ñg ñg "to "aaa" as one approaches the point in the right nostril before once again progressing toward the point in the left nostril.

**8.** Continue the circuit while smoothly transitioning the sounds and vibration of the mantra until the points and the lines between the points begin to light up.

**9.** As the triangle begins to light up, imagery may appear in the interior of the triangle. Another effect may be that a field of color begins to establish itself in one's awareness. Tactilely, a razor thin plane of awareness may develop between the indentation above the upper lip, through the tip and bridge of the nose, extending to the apex of the triangle located in the center of the forehead. All of these subtle sensations result from beginning to balance the right and left energies.

**10.** Rather than use the points of step two, one can use the following points. This can be particularly useful if one has anatomical variants or medical conditions that make focusing on the flow of the breath in the nostrils more difficult.

a. Right point = center of the pupil, or energetic center of the orbit of the right eye.

b. Left point = center of the pupil, or energetic center of the orbit of the left eye.

c. Apex = the gateway of trikuti cakra roughly located in the center of the forehead.

**11.** Once one has practiced with the triangles of step two and/or step ten, a third triangle that can be used is:

a. Right point = energetic point associated with the meatus (opening) of the right ear.

b. Left point = energetic point associated with the meatus of the left ear.

c. Apex = an interior point within the skull located under the vertex (externally, the point of the skull closest to the ceiling when one is seated or standing). As one balances the right and left energies, this point under the vertex of the skull can begin to light up.

**12.** As the points and lines of this interior triangle begin to light up, focus on the area midway between the right point and the left point. In this area will be an interior junction point of iḍā, piṅgalā, and suṣumṇa. Becoming familiar with this point will assist one in such practices as aum kriya and śītalī karaṇa where the awareness seeks to follow the flow of energy through this point without restriction.

Once the right and left energies have come to balance and the gateway on the forehead shows itself, the challenge is to let one's awareness through the gateway while maintaining the balance between iḍā and piṅgalā. The key to both of the following methods is to maintain steadiness while making the transition. The fluctuations of the mind can easily interrupt the process if the mind has not yet become simply a tool of consciousness.

### *Piercing Trikuti Cakra*

One goal of moving through the gateway of trikuti cakra is to enter the nādī that leads to the choices offered at the internal junction of iḍā, piṅgalā, and suṣumṇa.

#### *Method One*

If a field of color emerges while balancing the energies at ājñā cakra, remain steady. This means not being fascinated or otherwise emotionally attached to the appearance of the color. If suṣumṇa awareness is maintained, the field of color may resolve in at least two ways and reveal what the veil of color was covering. The first way is that the field of color may organize itself into lotus petals and open up centrally. Another way is that the refinement of gaze of the observer may seemingly approach the field of color and begin to distinguish its true nature. When observed closely, a field of color is actually a pattern of light. Within the pattern are dark areas. It is much like a screen door, which from a distance may appear uniform, but as one gets closer to the screen, one notices the pattern of holes in the screen. If suṣumṇa awareness is maintained, the practitioner's awareness moves through a hole in the screen, a dark space in the pattern, and experiences what lies beyond the veil.

#### *Method Two*

Practitioners who are more visually oriented may wish to examine the practice given many years ago by my teacher, Swami Rama, during a week-long seminar titled "Saundaryalahari".

**1.** Visualize the following image of ājñā cakra with a petal on either side of a central circle.

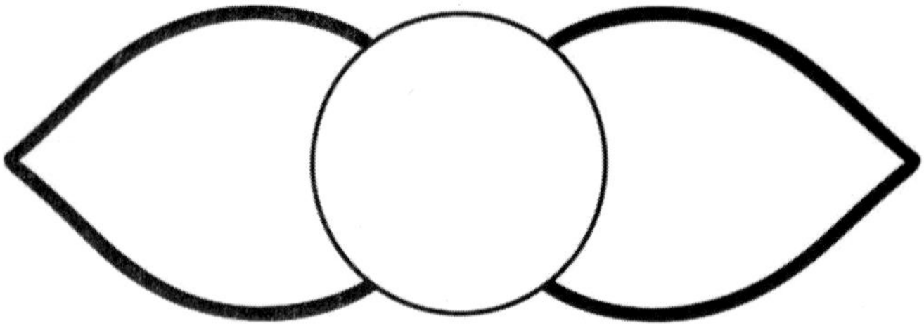

**2.** Within the circle of color or light between the petals, create the image of or simply focus on a dark space.

As with the preceding method number one, if suṣumṇa application is maintained one is then able to move into the subtleties of the internal energetic system.

It has been my experience that anytime iḍā and piṅgalā have been sufficiently balanced to establish and maintain suṣumṇa awareness, the force of grace in the world manifests in various ways and forms to help assist me in my exploration of the subtleties of my being.

The relationship of ājñā cakra to saṃskāras, the seed mantra "soḥaṃ", and the mind will be dealt with in a subsequent chapter.

### *Something to consider:*

Ājñā has different translations depending on the source. The root word "jñā" means "to know". Ajñā, an alternative spelling of ājñā, can mean "not to know, or no knowledge." It took a long time for me to realize that through practice my teacher wanted me to take my mind to a state where it would "know nothing". With that fresh slate of silence, or knowing nothing, consciousness could perceive without the influence of the impressions residing in the conscious or unconscious mind.

## Anāhata Cakra

The triangle technique used in balancing the right and left energies at ājñā cakra can also be used with anāhata cakra. Anāhata cakra is often depicted as an intersecting upward and downward triangle.

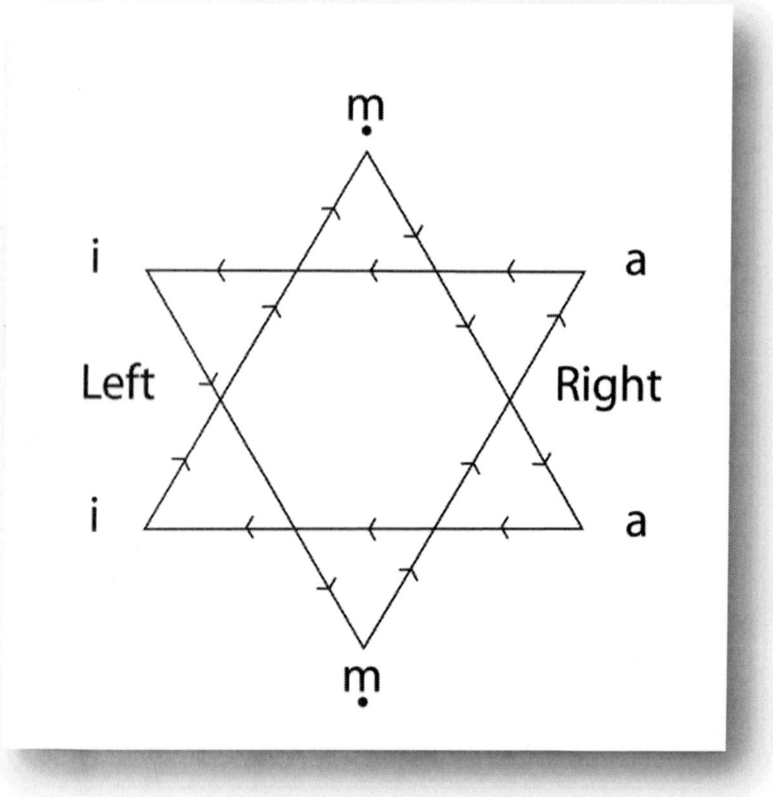


One will note that when using the following technique to trace the triangles with the mantra "aiṃ" that the upward facing triangle in this diagram is followed in a clockwise direction, and the downward facing triangle is followed in a counter-clockwise direction.

*Triangles and Anāhata Cakra*

**1.** If one wishes to use a smaller set of triangles, one can use the following energy points:

Downward triangle:

a. Right point = tip of the right nipple.

b. Left point = tip of the left nipple.

c. Apex = navel.

**Upward triangle:**

a. Right point = an energy point in the liver located under the right hypochondrium (portion of the abdomen located under the right lower anterior ribs).

b. Left point = an energy point in the area of the spleen located under the left hypochondrium.

c. Apex = thymus gland under the sternum, or alternatively, the energy point within the radiance of the throat cakra at the jugular notch located just superior to the upper border of the sternum.

If one wishes to use a larger set of triangles, the practitioner can use the following:

**Downward triangle:**

a. Right point = right shoulder.

b. Left point= left shoulder.

c. Apex = any centrally located energy point of svādiṣṭhāna or mūlādhāra cakra. Examples of such energy points would be the pubic symphysis, base of the shaft of the clitoris or penis, anus, or CV-1.

**Upward triangle:**

a. Right point = right hip or right hip pointer (anterior superior iliac spine).

b. Left point = left hip or left anterior superior iliac spine.

c. Apex = radiance of ājñā cakra between the eyes or gateway of trikuti cakra on the center of the forehead.

**2.** As with the practice of using triangles and the mantra "aiṃ" at ājñā cakra, one begins by selecting the right point of either the upward or downward triangle and placing the vibration of "aaa" at that point. Draw the vibration of the sound across the base of the triangle toward the left point. Make certain the vibration of the mantra merges with the right point before beginning to draw the vibration towards the left point.

**3.** As one approaches the left point, gradually transition the sound of "aaa" to "iii" (pronounced "eee") as one moves the awareness through the left point and proceeds toward the apex.

**4.** As one approaches the apex, transition the sound and vibration to "ṃṃṃ" or "ñg ñg ñg" as one moves the awareness through the apex and continues toward the right point.

**5.** Smoothly transition from "ṃṃṃ" or "ñg ñg ñg" to "aaa" as one approaches the right point.

**6.** Continue the circuit while smoothly transitioning the sounds and vibration of the mantra until the points and the lines between the points begin to light up.

**7.** Repeat steps two through six with the other intersecting triangle.

**8.** Once one has been able to bring both triangles clearly into one's awareness, perform steps two through six simultaneously with both triangles. The test of focus during this step will be for the practitioner to maintain awareness as the lines of the triangles cross.

**9.** As the right and left energies of piṅgalā and iḍā begin to balance with this technique, an invitation to attend to the radiance defined by the intersection of the two triangles can be felt. Once the invitation to attend to the central radiance has been received, it is generally best to honor that invitation rather than trying to continue the triangle practice.

Following are three practices a practitioner might find useful while attending to the central radiance of the intersecting energetic triangles.

### *"Soḥaṃ" at Anāhata Cakra*

If one has already established focus within the central radiance of the intersection of the triangles, and one is already familiar with the energetic points of hṛt and dvādaṣāṅta, skip steps one through seven and begin with step eight. If the energetic point of hṛt within the central radiance of anāhata cakra is not familiar to the practitioner, the following steps one through seven can help establish familiarity with that energetic point.

**1.** Establish diaphragmatic breathing.

**2.** Attend to the flow of the breath in the nostrils, feeling the coolness on the inhale and the warmth on the exhale.

**3.** Balance the left and the right prāṇas, allowing the right and left nostrils to flow equally.

**4.** Find a stream of coolness in each nostril, feeling two distinct streams of cool air flow on inhalation, one in each nostril.

**5.** As you inhale, follow the two streams of coolness to an area of joining deep in the nasal cavity. Spend a few breaths sensing the transitions between warmth on the exhale and coolness on the inhale at that area of joining. This is one area where the mantra "soḥaṃ" may begin to whisper to you. This region is in close proximity to the internal junction of iḍā, piṅgalā, and suṣumnā.

**6.** During inhalation follow that coolness inward and downward to the area of the larynx. At any time during the practice, one can merge the mantra "soḥaṃ" with the breath. Spend a few breaths in the area of the larynx sensing the temperature changes on inhalation and exhalation. Look for the exact moments of temperature change to deepen the focus.

**7.** Now, inhale and follow the coolness down to the deepest point. If the diaphragmatic contraction is complete, your tactile awareness will be led near an energy point called hṛt (hrit) deep within anāhata cakra. Spend a few breaths focusing on this point.

**8.** Four finger widths anterior to the area of the thorax where the lowest ribs join the sternum, there is another energy point called dvādaṣāṅta. Exhale from the energy point hṛt into the radiance of anāhata cakra to dvādaṣāṅta. Inhale back to hṛt. Continue to merge the mantra "soḥaṃ" with the breath.

**9.** Merge the vibration of the mantra "soḥaṃ" with the subtle sensations of the prāṇa flow between hṛt and dvādaṣāṅta. This step nine is one of the 112 practices from the text Vijñāna Bhairāva, though the mantra "soḥaṃ" is not given in that text for this practice.

### *Seed Mantra at Anāhata Cakra*

The seed mantra, or bīja mantra, of anāhata cakra is "yam". When focusing on the vibration of a bīja mantra at the four lower cakras, the vibratory nature of the associated element with each of those cakras can be connected to the initial sound of the bīja mantra. When an initial vibration of the consonant "y" is extended by the vowel "a", the texture of the element air becomes the vibration associated with a breeze or wind passing through a particular space.

**1.** Focus on the radiance of the intersection of the two triangles of anāhata cakra after establishing diaphragmatic breathing.

**2.** During the initial exhalation, follow the flow of prāṇa anteriorly. Merge the vibration of the sound of a breeze or wind with the flow.

**3.** During inhalation, draw the flow of prāṇa into the radiance of the intersection and follow it posteriorly, essentially moving the flow completely through the central portion of the cakra from anterior to posterior.

**4.** During exhalation, draw the flow of prāṇa from behind the radiance, through the central radiance, and follow the flow anteriorly. Keep the vibration of the bīja mantra merged with the flow.

**5.** Within the area of central radiance, the center point of the cakra can light up and invite the practitioner's attention. When this occurs, merge the vibration of all of the sounds and textures of the bīja mantra with that center point. As with any cakra that may begin to reveal its teachings, the force of grace may show itself in various forms and ways.

### *Listening for the Unstruck Sound*

Balancing the flows of a cakra can lead to an invitation to attend to absolute silence. Listening to the silence can help one understand the origin of vibration that we call manifestation or creation. The union of infinite potential and the force of manifestation occurs in absolute silence. If one attends to that absolute silence with unbroken awareness, one can experience with the subtle senses the vibration that first emerges from that union.

What is required for unbroken awareness is citta-vṛtti-nirodha, silence of the waves of the mind. In a later chapter we will look at the nature of the saṃskāras, impressions in the mind, and how they can interrupt unbroken awareness. We will then examine approaches and practices to help limit the influence of saṃskāras when trying to take one's awareness to silence.

### ***Something to Consider:***

Reading words from scripture or mentally repeating words and sounds of a mantra without bhakti and connecting those words and phrases to the heart energy of reverence and devotion can cause the words of scripture and mantras to ring hollow in the mind. The practice of chanting bhajans or kirtan can help to engage bhakti in other aspects of one's yoga practice.

## Mūlādhāra Cakra

### *Modifying the Flow of Mūlādhāra Cakra*

Mūlādhāra cakra offers another method by which to balance the flows of prāṇa at a cakra. The following method uses the balancing of lateral flows related to the cakra in order to bring the central gateway of the cakra into view.

**1.** Define the space within which to do the work.

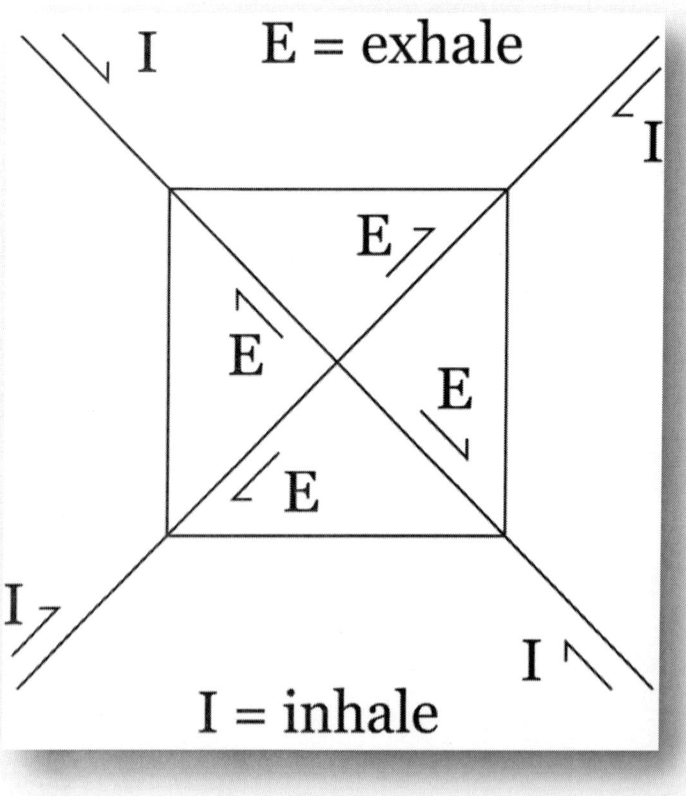


The outer edges of the small square are the ischial tuberosities (sit bones that rest upon the ground in meditation postures). Define the sides of the square first before adding the anterior and posterior borders of the square. Viewpoint of the foregoing drawing is as if one is looking downward at one's perineum. To accentuate awareness, it can be helpful to put a cushion under the perineum to support the area, just as one might support the area during vigorous prāṇayāma practice.

**2.** Establish even diaphragmatic breathing while maintaining an erect seated posture.

**3.** Balance the flow of the nostrils as much as possible before moving awareness downward to the area of the perineum between the ischial tuberosities (sit bones).

**4.** Once the sides of the square in step one are defined, exhale with awareness of the lateral flow of prāṇa from the center point through the anterior corners. Then inhale back through the anterior corners to the center point and somewhat up the central channel. Try not to imagine the flow, but simply follow it. Attend to both left and right corner flows with exactly equal intensity of focus.

**5.** Merge the vibration of the mantra "soḥaṃ" with the flow of the prāṇa during exhalation and inhalation.

**6.** Repeat steps four and five, but this time focusing on the flow of prāṇa through the two posterior corners.

**7.** Now study the lateral flow in time with the breath through all four corners simultaneously with exactly equal intensity of focus applied to each of the four flows

**8.** Continue focusing on the flow until the left and right energies (iḍā and piṅgalā) are sufficiently balanced to have the center point of the cakra begin to light up and invite the attention of the mind.

**9.** When the center point lights up, one can use the bīja mantra of mūlādhāra cakra to tease the gateway. The seed mantra is "lam" (pronounced “lum” as in “lump”), with the texture of the earth element resonating with the initial consonant "l" and activation of that texture related to the "a" sound of the mantra. The texture is like the slight but solid thud of a lump of earth or sand dropped onto the ground.

If the subtle upward and downward rhythm that accompanies the subtle prāṇa flow associated with the body's craniorespiratory rhythm can be felt, merge the initial sound of the bīja mantra with the downward flow of that rhythm. Merge the remaining vowel sounds of the mantra with the upward flow.

## Maṇipūra Cakra

### *Modifying the Flow of Maṇipūra Cakra*

The technique of balancing the lateral prāṇa flows used in the last chapter with mūlādhāra cakra can also be applied to maṇipūra cakra. Before trying to balance the lateral flows through all ten lotus petals, it is helpful to first become aware of the lateral flow through the navel. Then adopt a visual image with which to assist the work.

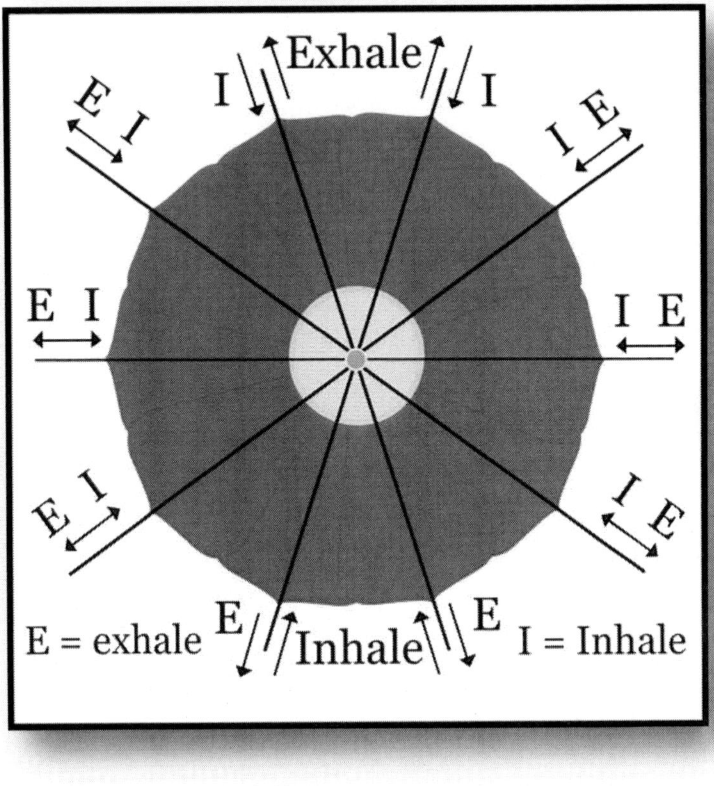


**1.** Begin by balancing the left and right flow at the nostrils until the invitation to attend to the energy at the tip of the nose or at the indentation above the upper lip begins to offer itself to your awareness.

**2.** As the energy channel leading downward comes into your awareness, follow it through the energy point at the center of the chin, downward behind the sternum, and follow the anterior channel to the navel.

**3.** Establish smooth diaphragmatic breathing while keeping the centermost point of the navel in your awareness.

**4.** Sense the lateral prāṇa flow moving outward through the center point of the navel during exhalation (the physical navel is drawn toward the spine during exhalation). Then sense the prāṇa flow moving inward through the center point during inhalation.

**5.** Merge the vibration of the mantra "soḥaṃ" with the flow through the navel.

**6.** Visualize the image of the cakra in a way that makes sense. Ten petals organized around a central flame is one way to visualize the cakra. Substituting embers or burning logs feeding the central fire is another method. Whichever image is used, locate that image behind the navel and let the gaze be from the perspective of looking downward at the image. The central base of the fire, as well as the tip of the flame should be on the center line that connects the center points of the major cakras.

**7.** One sequence for balancing the prāṇa flow is as follows.

a. Exhale with the lateral flow through 2 anterior petals or embers (one petal left and one petal right of the anterior midline). Inhale back through the petals to the center point at the base of the flame and upward. Merge the vibration of the mantra "soḥaṃ" with the flow. Keep in mind the texture of the element agni associated with maṇipūra cakra not only has heat associated with fire, but also has the capacity for illumination, or light. Merge the texture of agni with the flow as well, moving outward through the embers with the exhale, and drawing prāṇa through the embers on the inhale, gathering the energy of the embers as you do so.

b. Repeat step "a" with the second pair of anterior petals.

c. Similarly work with the first pair of posterior petals or embers.

d. Then work with the second pair of posterior petals.

e. Merge the flow of prāṇa with the two lateral embers or petals.

f. Merge the flow with the 4 anterior petals.

g. Merge the flow with the four posterior petals.

h. Merge the flow with all 10 petals or embers.

**8.** When the central gateway at the base of the flame invites your attention, begin the repetition of the bīja mantra "ram". The texture of the flame is contained in the rolling "r" and the activation of the texture begins with the 2nd sound "a". Place the vibration of the sounds at the center point at the base of the flame. The sound of the bīja mantra can have the force that one feels upon opening the door of a blast furnace, or it may be nearly silent as if one's ear is held close to a candle flame. If the sounds of the mantra are lengthened to respond to the gentle upward and downward rhythm (following the cranio-respiratory rhythm) at the center point, the sounds of the mantra "ram" may lengthen and become "ṝṝṝāāāṃṃṃ". This change in pronunciation resembles the way another mantra such as "soḥaṃ" can become "ssooḥḥāāṃṃ" as it merges into the flow of prāṇa.

**9.** As with mūlādhāra cakra, use the subtle upward and downward rhythm that accompanies the cranio-respiratory rhythm to tease the gateway.

**10.** The invitation to enter the gateway is accompanied by an invitation to silence. Do not ignore the invitation by continuing to actively repeat mantra japa, or you may miss the opening of the gateway and the invitation to enter the subtle realm of the self.

# Viśuddha Cakra

First a word about ākāśa, the element of the throat cakra. The element ākāśa is usually translated as space or ether. The texture of ākāśa is absence of vibration, absolute silence. Before ākāśa accepts a vibration, it is a perfectly balanced sum of all the forces in the entire universe. Some physicists describe it as having infinite energy density. In other words, once ākāśa accepts the vibration of a combination of the textures of the elements of earth, fire, water, and air, ākāśa then has the potential to manifest as any vibration. Space that was perceived by the senses to be an empty void then has the potential to become absolutely anything.

So where is ākāśa? The answer is that it is everywhere that has not yet accepted a vibration to become manifest. The imagery often suggested as a practice for this cakra is a blue sky with a full moon. To focus on the texture of ākāśa, focus on the emptiness of space between the sky of this earth and the moon rather than focusing on the sky or the moon. Unmanifest space can be anywhere, including within what we perceive with our gross senses to be something manifest. Ether is present between and also within the minute energetic entities that we call particles of atoms.

***Something to consider:***

Most of what we perceive to be solids, liquids, and gases is made of up predominately unmanifest space, capable of transmuting or transforming into virtually anything upon simply accepting a vibratory influence. In ayurveda, ākāśa is considered to be vāta. In pure form ākāśa is absolutely still, yet ākāśa can accept any pattern of vibration and be influenced to become anything.

### *Balancing Iḍā and Piṅgalā at Viśuddha Cakra*

To balance the energies of viśuddha cakra, one can make use of the side-to-side dance of iḍā and piṅgalā.

**1.** Establish diaphragmatic breathing and balance the left and right energy at ājñā cakra.

**2.** As the central channel comes into view, become aware of the dance between iḍā and piṅgalā at the indentation above the upper lip. As the energy sweeps side to side, equalize the amplitude to each side.

**3.** Follow the central channel offered downward through the center of the chin and behind the superior aspect of the sternum in the area just below the pit of the throat. There is a very quiet space behind the upper sternum (manubrium) where one can focus on the quality of absolute stillness.

**4.** Sense the side-to-side rhythm of the dance, initially through the area of the pit of the throat. Follow the dance side-to-side between the junctions of the collar bones (clavicles) and the manubrium (upper segment of sternum). Equalize the amplitude of the energetic dance to each side while following the rhythm of the dance.

**5.** Extend the rhythm of the dance through the shoulders to each side, again with equal amplitude to both the right and the left.

### *Use of the Bīja Mantra at Viśuddha Cakra*

**1.** The seed mantra of viśuddha cakra is "Ham" (English pronunciation “hum”), which translates as "That" where "That" means all that is. Remember the element ākāśa is capable of accepting the texture of a vibration pattern and is capable of manifesting into anything. The mantra "Ham" has three sounds, "hhh", "aaa", and "mmm". Rather than mentally repeating the mantra "Ham", find the sound of the three sounds that most resonates with the mind. Practice maintaining each of the sounds "ḥḥḥ", "āāā" or "mmm" or “” ṃṃṃ for as long as the mind can keep each of the sounds resonating in the mind before changing focus. The sound that the mind can best hold continuously in awareness without distraction is a sound to use with the following practice.

**2.** Bring the awareness to the quiet space behind the sternum and gently intone the vibration of the chosen sound into that stillness.

**3.** Alternatively, one can simply focus on the quality of stillness within that space, as silence is the fourth sound that follows the audible three sounds of the mantra.

Continuous focus on any of the individual sounds "ḥḥḥ", "āāā", "ṃṃṃ” (or “mmm") are three of the 112 practices from the Vijñāna Bhairāva. The purpose of those 112 practices are to enlist the aid of the Śhaktis in one's endeavors, including the deepening of awareness in one's yoga practice.

## Svādiṣṭhāna Cakra

Svādiṣṭhāna cakra practices offer a unique challenge for the practitioner. When the "ha" and the "tha" come into perfect balance and suṣumṇa is established, the resulting suṣumṇa application can trigger a sexual orgasm. For this reason, many schools of yoga do not teach practices involving svādiṣṭhāna cakra. The challenge for the practitioner in working with the energetics of this cakra is to remain focused on the energetic work rather than allowing the mind to follow the sexual sensations. Working with svādiṣṭhāna cakra presents an opportunity to train the mind to become a tool of consciousness rather than having the mind lead consciousness.

### *Balancing Iḍā and Piṅgalā at Svādiṣṭhāna Cakra*

Svādiṣṭhāna cakra can be depicted as a circle containing a crescent moon.

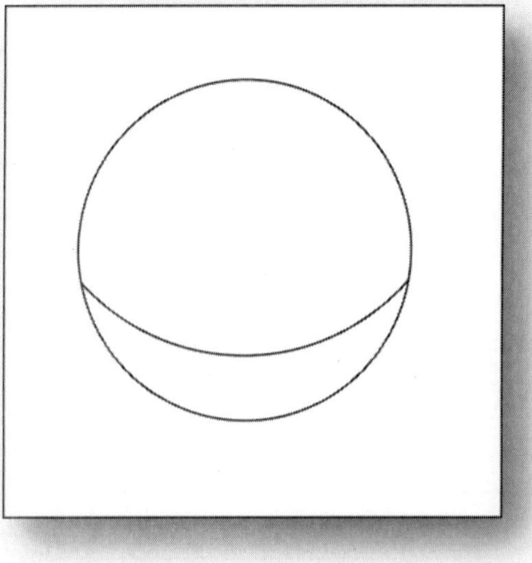

The crescent moon is actually a support for a globe of water represented by the circle. Supporting the water is a bowl resembling moisture coated white porcelain, roughly in the area of the pelvic floor. The water is not stationary, but actually has fluidity and movement. The water also is not bound by a skin as a balloon full of water might be. The center point of focus of the cakra is at the very base of the bowl.

**1.** The first challenge is to tactilely sense the area related to the cakra. As with other cakras, balance the nostril flow at the nasal area and begin to sense the energy channel that extends downward from the indentation above the upper lip. This anterior channel downward is known in the Taoist tradition as the conception channel. Follow the channel downward past the indentation in the tip of the chin, behind the sternum, through the anterior radiance of the anāhata cakra, past the navel and into the region of svādiṣṭhāna cakra.

**2.** Become aware of the bowl. The ASIS (anterior superior iliac spines, or hip pointers that are part of the pelvis) are useful landmarks to define the right and left region within which to focus.

**3.** Sweep the energy through the pelvic bowel from hip pointer to hip pointer, churning the globe of water until a pattern of current and flow are established. Make the amplitude of the force and current to each side be equal. Do this until the energetic gateway at the base of the bowl begins to light up, indicating that iḍā and piṅgalā are beginning to balance at the cakra.

### *Use of the Bīja Mantra at Svādiṣṭhāna Cakra*

**1.** Once the energetic gateway at the center of the bowl is in awareness (step three of the previous practice), begin intoning the vibration of the seed mantra "vam", infusing the vibration of the mantra into the gateway. Keep in mind the "v" sound is like a buzzing "w" or "vw" (see pronunciation guide). When the texture of the "v" is activated by "a" (pronounced as the "u" in the English word "hum"), then "vam" resembles the sound of an ocean breaker coming into the beach. This is the texture of the water element associated with the cakra. The vibration of the sounds of the bīja mantra may start to follow a pattern of gentle upward and downward flow of prāṇa through the center point. That flow times with the cranio-respiratory rhythm.

**2.** One may also want to do some energetic clearing between this gateway and other physical and energetic connections to svādiṣṭhāna cakra. Using the mantra "soḥaṃ" exhale from the center point through the perceived structure (testes, ovaries, uterus, prostate, kidneys, bladder, lower extremities), and inhale back through the structures to the gateway and up the central channel.

### *Energy Clearing and Energy Cultivation*

Once clearing the energy through the associated structures has been completed, one may wish to begin to cultivate and gather the energies associated with svādiṣṭhāna cakra. Cultivation is a twofold process. One offers the energy of the cakra to associated energies of the anatomical structures (ovaries or testes, for example), and gathers the energies from the structures back into the cakra on the inhale. This type of clearing and cultivation can be practiced at any cakra and the subtle energies of associated anatomical structures.

### *Cultivating Circuits Related to Svādiṣṭhāna Cakra*

Activating the prāṇas associated with svādiṣṭhāna cakra without cultivation can lead to stagnation of energy. Stagnation of energy in any area ultimately leads to imbalance, loss of vitality to associated structures of a cakra, and ultimately to loss of vitality of the individual and death.

**1.** Center the awareness in the energy of svādiṣṭhāna cakra.

**2.** Exhale downward through the radiance, exiting the pelvic floor at the energetic point associated with the base of the shaft of the penis or clitoris.

**3.** Loop the energy during the transition between exhalation and inhalation and re-enter the pelvic floor at the energy point midway between the posterior opening of the vaginal canal and the anus (CV-1 in oriental medicine terms). For males this point will be approximately ½ to 1 inch anterior to the anus on the surface of the perineum.

**4.** Continue to follow the energy upward posteriorly (governing channel) with an inhalation upward into the posterior radiance of svādiṣṭhāna cakra.

**5.** During the transition between inhalation and exhalation, loop the energy anteriorly before following it downward through the conception channel as in step two.

**6.** Continue this cycle until the looping is comfortable and steady.

**7.** Once comfortable with step six, continue the inhalation up the posterior governing channel to maṇipūra cakra. Then loop anteriorly and exhale downward through the conception channel. Looping the energy as in step three, continue the circuit timed with the breath.

**8.** Once comfortable looping the three cakras, add anāhata cakra into the loop. Be patient with this practice. It may take some time to be comfortable looping without losing focus. If cakras are skipped in the cultivation process, go back to a previous step until awareness can be sustained and all cakras in the loop remain included.

**9.** Add viśuddha cakra and ājñā cakra into the loop as comfort with the practice develops. When looping at ājñā cakra, enter posteriorly at the central base of the skull. Traverse through the junction of iḍā, piṅgalā, and suṣumnā near the pituitary gland at the center of the skull. Then exit anteriorly at the space between the eyebrows.

**10.** Eventually follow the energy channel on the inhale posteriorly to the area of sahasrāra. Loop the energy forward to the energy point at the space between the eyebrow during the transition between inhalation and exhalation. During the loop, include the energy point within sahasrāra just under the vertex of the skull as well as the gateway point of trikuti cakra.

**11.** Exhale downward through the plane of energy between the gateway point of trikuti cakra, through the bridge of the nose, to the tip of the nose, and to the indentation above the upper lip. Continue the exhalation downward through the anterior conception channel.

One may wish to add the vibration of a mantra into the energetic flow, drawing the vibration of each sound along with the flow in each phase of the circuit. "Soḥaṃ" or other mantras may be used for this purpose. Try to use mantras that time well with the breath such as "AUM". If using "AUM", for example, time the transition of sounds as one would in the practice of Aum kriya, namely transitioning to the "uuu" sound as one approaches and passes the throat cakra. On both the upward and the downward journey, transition to "aaa" from the "mmm" or "ṃṃṃ" sound as one loops the energy circuit during transitions in phases of the breath.

Once energy of the cakra has been cultivated and gathered, it is wise to make use of it in some way. Stagnation of flow or excess of energy at any cakra can produce imbalance, and svādiṣṭhāna cakra is no different in that regard. Some suggestions regarding this are:

**1.** To gather the cultivated energy of svādiṣṭhāna cakra for use in activities involving heartfelt love and compassion (healing work, selfless prayer, etc.), end the circuit during downward exhalation at the heart cakra for several cycles instead of continuing to traverse the entire circuit. At the heart cakra, one finishes each of the final few exhalations by exhaling into the radiance of the cakra. Remember that the radiance of a cakra can extend in all directions.

**2.** For more active work, including seva (service), end the cultivation circuit during downward exhalation by exhaling into the radiance of maṇipūra cakra for several cycles.

**3.** For intimacy, there are practices with a partner that can be shared. A few of these practices are presented in the following chapter.

# Cultivation of Energy with a Partner

Part of the challenge for a yoga practitioner as capacity for awareness expands is to remain energetically balanced no matter what the experience. Learning to be intimate and share with another is a training ground for learning to be in balance with awareness of everyone and everything. If as a yoga practitioner, the goal is to realize the Divine within oneself, to have knowledge of the infinite, it makes some sense to practice harmonizing in a relationship with a partner in life. If one cannot be in harmony with another human being, how can one expect to be in harmony with the infinite. While human relationships are not the only way to practice being in harmony and energetic balance, such relationships do present opportunities to practice balance with intimacy.

## *Sharing Energy at Anāhata Cakra: Method One*

**1.** Position yourself so that you are facing your partner with an erect spine. Having each other's heart cakra at the same height from the floor is helpful, but not essential for learning the practice.

**2.** While being physically joined is not necessary, having a comfortable proximity is helpful. As the partner exhales the energy anteriorly, one should be close enough to sense it.

**3.** Become aware of the radiance of anāhata cakra at the intersection of the two triangles, balancing left and right energies as much as possible.

**4.** Exhale anteriorly into the radiance and through the radiance of your partner's heart cakra. At the same time, the partner should inhale from behind the area of your heart cakra and draw the energy through their radiance. Essentially, you and your partner are moving energy in the same direction of flow through both cakras while each partner is engaging opposite phases of the breath. As you exhale, he or she inhales, and vice versa. Match the rate of the breath and smoothly move the energy through both heart centers with each phase of the breath.

**5.** Once you are able to easily sense the joining of rhythms, you may wish to position behind your partner and practice moving the energy through both heart centers while exhaling and inhaling at the same time as your partner.

**6.** Other positions may be tried, including those of physical intimacy if desired. Sexual stimulation can either enhance or distract one from attending to the energetics.

### *Sharing Energy at Anāhata Cakra: Method Two*

**1.** Position yourselves as in method one.

**2.** Become aware of the side to side dance between iḍā and piṅgalā, first with yourself and then find your partner's rhythm. Perception of prāṇa should be second nature at some point if you have been practicing the offerings of this text.

**3.** Match the right and left dance with your partner.

### *Sharing the Cultivation Circuit of Svādiṣṭhāna Cakra*

**1.** Position yourself so that you are facing your partner with an erect spine.

**2.** Focus on the cultivation circuit with as many cakras as mutually agreed upon. (See the section "Cultivating the Circuits Related to Svādiṣṭhāna Cakra" in the previous chapter.) When practicing with a partner, match your inhalation with their exhalation and your exhalation with their inhalation. This has the effect of influencing the downward flow in the conception channel of your partner during your exhalation while your partner is focusing on their posterior governing channel during their inhalation.

**3.** This method may also be practiced during sexual union or in different positions, though the effect on the partner's flow may be different than that of step two, particularly if partners are not face to face.

## Sahasrāra Cakra

The study of sahasrāra cakra can lead to profound insight such as being able to witness the union of Śakti and Śiva in the process of creation. The study of this cakra may also lead to an understanding of an aspect of the cakra called Saundaryalahari, the ocean of beauty or ocean of bliss. As the name implies, the view of Saundaryalahari (an interior view of sahasrāra cakra) is intensely beautiful and blissful.

To experience the full beauty and bliss of this cakra requires the application of suṣumṇa awareness following the perfect balance of energies of iḍā and piṅgalā. However, there are methods of practice which can help build familiarity with this cakra so that one may incorporate the experience of this cakra during practices involving multiple cakras.

### *Sources of Brilliance Related to Sahasrāra Cakra*

There are multiple areas of brilliance within the region of sahasrāra cakra. It is worth spending some time studying these areas of brilliance and noticing their relationships with each other.

#### *Method One*

**1.** As in the study of ājñā cakra, allowing the junction of iḍā, piṅgalā and suṣumṇa deep within the skull to light up can help with the focus on aspects of sahasrāra cakra. As this internal junction of ājñā cakra lights up, look for an area of brilliance under the vertex of the skull. The vertex is the area of the skull that is closest to the ceiling as one is standing. Study the energetic relationship between these two sources of brilliance.

**2.** Intone the vibration of the seed mantra "Hamsa" into the area of brilliance under the vertex of the skull. Pay special attention to smoothing out the transitions between each sound of the mantra. Inhaling to the sound of "Ham" and exhaling to the sound of "sa" is one way to time the breath with the vibration. Some may choose to reverse the phase of the breath with the sounds. Regardless of how the breath is timed with the sounds, make the transitions between phases of the breath as well as transitions between each sound perfectly smooth.

### *Method Two*

**1.** Become aware of an area of brilliance inside the upper portion of the central forehead. Study the relationship between this area of brilliance and the internal junction of iḍā, piṅgalā and suṣumṇa located in the center of the skull. One can simply study the relationship between the two areas, or one can look for the flow between the two areas of brilliance that relates to the breath rhythm.

**2.** To smooth the flow between these two areas, intone the seed mantra "soḥaṃ" into the flow that is timed with the breath. During inhalation, the vibration and flow may move into the junction of iḍā, piṅgalā and suṣumṇa and then travel upward toward the illumination under the vertex of the skull. During exhalation, the flow may move through the area of brilliance behind the upper forehead.

There are many energy centers on the surface and within the area of the skull. If one takes into account the number of petals of sahasrāra cakra, or the number of waves of the ocean in Saundaryalahari, the number of potential energy centers may be infinite.

One energy center that different traditions talk about is soma cakra. Different traditions locate this cakra in different areas within sahasrāra cakra. Some locate it between the internal junction of iḍā, piṅgalā and suṣumṇa and the vertex of the skull. Others locate it more anteriorly, closer to the interior aspect of the forehead. Some traditions define soma cakra as two cakras with a bridge between. Traditions also may suggest different visualizations, such as illuminated light-blue lotus petals, 12 or 16 in number. As with any visualization of a cakra, the practitioner's personal experience of the cakra will supersede any prior description provided by any tradition. Different traditions also may recommend practice of particular mantras once soma cakra is experienced. For this practitioner, intoning the vibration of the mantra within the cakra with focused attention seems to lead to a better balance of energies than trying to repeat the mantra or mantras many times with a more cognitive focus. The quality of repetition seems more important than the number of repetitions.

## Samāyā Tantra and the Mind

Before understanding the nature of saṃskāras, it is helpful to review the nature of the mind and its relationship to its origins and further manifestations. What follows is a section from the book Practical Yoga Sutras, by this author. My teacher would draw the diagram below in many of his lectures to help explain the relationship between soul, body and mind, and the interface of prāṇa and kuṇḍalinī.

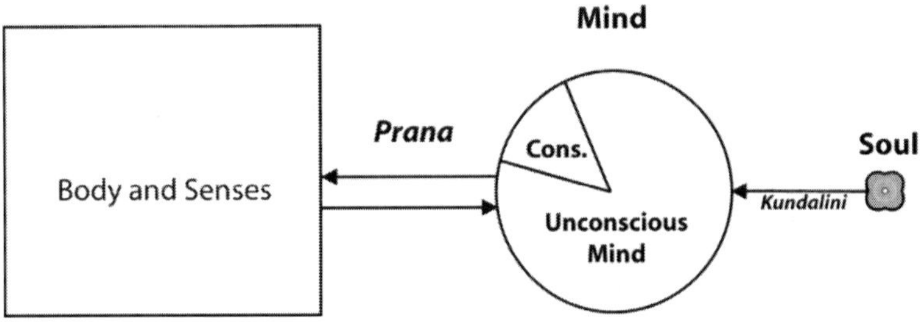


During one of his lectures my teacher was asked to define the soul. He explained that if you take a spark of divine potential and wrap it in layers and layers of ignorance you then have a human soul. If you then apply the force of kuṇḍalinī (first prāṇa, Śakti, Divine Mother, Holy Spirit, silver cord) through the layers of ignorance (influenced by past karmas), the mind is created. The energies of prāṇa then further act as an interface between the mind and the body and senses.

One aspect of the mind is citta-vṛitti. This is considered a storehouse of the vibrations of the universe. The physicists of the world will tell us that this printed page or a computer screen upon which it may be viewed is merely a collection of molecules. These molecules are made up of atoms. The atoms are made up of particles of atoms. The particles, upon closer examination, are nothing but organizations of energy and vibration of different wavelengths. Depending upon how the energetic vibrations are organized within a particular space, that space can be perceived by our senses in different ways, such as solids, liquids, gases, a printed page, or as virtually anything.

The mystics of different traditions tell us that all phenomena, all events, all objects in the universe have a vibratory nature and that each vibration radiates everywhere in the universe. Every phenomena, event, word uttered, or thought, is projected throughout the entire universe and registered in the mind as either a conscious or an unconscious experience. If a tree falls in the forest and we are in our homes, the tree falling registers as a subtle vibration in our unconscious. If we are next to the tree when it falls, however, the event of the tree falling not only registers as a conscious experience but may also persist in our memory banks on an unconscious level.

What defines us as individual human beings is the placement of the boundaries between the conscious and unconscious mind. While we may share similar conscious vibrations with another individual, having shared the same experience of being next to the tree when it fell, for example, there are differences of what registers on a conscious level for each human being. The totality of the conscious and unconscious mind, the totality of the circle of the mind in my teacher's diagram, is exactly the same for each and every one of us. It is the boundaries between conscious and unconscious mind that differ from individual to individual. We are indeed all created equal in that the totality of our mind is the same for each and every one of us. It is our awareness of the boundaries between conscious and unconscious mind that contributes to our perception of ourselves as individuals. That perception of our self as an individual is called ego or ahaṃkāra, our sense of I-am-ness.

Two of the eight limbs of yoga are designed to limit the influence of the mind on consciousness, and to facilitate the mind becoming the tool of consciousness. The yamas (attitudes of the mind) and niyamas (observances in daily life) are formulated to minimize the level of prāṇa attached to those saṃskāras, (impressions in the mind) left by thought, word, and deed.

Different cultures tend to develop different interpretations and rules related to the basic attitudes and observances in life. Individuals may also interpret the same action differently. For example, a parent may take a loaded gun away from a young child to protect the child and others. The child, however, may view the removal of the gun as an act of stealing and assume the parent is simply acting on a desire of acquisitiveness, or greed. Taking the time to gently educate the child about the potential dangers and/or benefits of a loaded gun may mitigate the energy attached to any saṃskāra related to the event.

Another set of actions subject to cultural interpretation is war. Some may order soldiers to go to war, or to use destructive weapons against people for reasons of greed to acquire wealth, control and power. Others may view the same acts of war as a necessary defense to preserve the values and people of a culture. The Bhagavad-Gita is very clear about the role of a yoga aspirant during times of war. Acts of war that appear to be violent may, at times, be necessary. Those necessary acts, however, are not for the pleasure of the actor. Vairāgya, or nonattachment, to thoughts, words, and deeds is key to not attaching energy of focus to saṃskāras that may interfere with the practitioner's progress toward the goal of yoga. Measuring responses to situations of life is key to my teacher's recommended practice for the yogi to "Grease everything you do with love."

Most saṃskāras are in the unconscious mind and are latent. There is no energy attached to the impressions that would allow them to continue influencing the mind. This is because most of the universe is outside of our boundaries of conscious awareness. Many impressions in the mind, however, result from thoughts, words, and deeds. In psychological terms, we call these saṃskāras "memories". What follows is a description of the components of memories. This description is taken from my book Practical Yoga Sutras. Following this description is a method of practice that can allow the practitioner to modify the influence of a saṃskāra on the mind.

"Memory has five components. For any event in the universe there is the knowledge of what happened that registers on either a conscious or an unconscious level. If a tree that falls over in the forest is observed to fall, the event registers on a conscious level and will still be present in one's unconscious memory bank even after the original event is forgotten.

There may be a behavior associated with the event. For example, one may have had to jump out of the way of the falling tree. This behavioral component also registers initially on a conscious level and later on an unconscious level. If one experienced fear that the tree falling might cause harm, then that feeling, or affect, will also register on a conscious and unconscious level. A tightening or grabbing sensation in the gut might accompany the fear. In addition to a visceral response to emotion, if one was actually hit by the tree there may be pain also associated with the experience as a bodily sensation.

Each event in the universe also has a prāṇic or vibratory component associated with it. The level of focus at the time of an event contributes to the amplitude of that vibratory, energetic component. In the above example, fear may have intensified one's concentration on the event of the tree falling.

An acronym, BAKES, for the components of memory is as follows:

**B**-behavior associated with the event.

**A**-affect associated with the event.

**K**-knowledge of what happened.

**E**-energetic component associated with the event.

**S**-bodily sensations associated with the event.

It is primarily the affect and energetic components associated with a memory that determines whether that event will continue to push forward in the mind and influence such states of the mind as a dream, conscious thinking, or the meditation practice of a practitioner."

## Modifying the Influence of Saṃskāras

Thoughts have locations. If you wish to observe this, count to 10 in the mind and note where you locate the impressions of those numbers. Most people locate thoughts such as this somewhere inside their skulls. Now lower the pitch significantly of that mental counting and notice any change in location of the impression. If the pitch is lowered enough, most will locate the impression somewhere in the thoracic area or lower. There will also tend to be a different sense, or feel, to the impression of that counting.

### *Changing the Locus of Vibration with AUM*

To experience the phenomena on a more concrete level, try audibly chanting the mantra "Aum". As you chant "aaa", "uuu", "mmm", note the difference in location of each of the sounds of the mantra.

Raise the pitch until producing the "mmm" sound of the mantra vibrates the cheekbones. Some may choose to raise the tongue slightly making "mmm" slightly nasal in character, "ṃṃṃ". Then lower the pitch until the "uuu" sound can be felt at the throat cakra or below.

### *Modifying Prāṇa Flow Through a Saṃskāra*

The lineage of teachers in the yoga traditions have noted that the cognitive component of a saṃskāra is most commonly associated with ājñā cakra. That is one reason ājñā cakra is often described as the seat of the mind.

Other aspects of an impression, such as affect or bodily sensations, may have a stronger association with other cakras. What follows is a practice using the natural flows of prāṇa with breath to modify the influence of a chosen saṃskāra.

**1.** The first step to modifying the influence of a saṃskāra on the mind is to locate the affinity of the saṃskāra to a location in space. While the energetic component of a saṃskāra radiates everywhere, the saṃskāra can have an affinity for a particular location in relationship to the mind.

**2.** When a particular saṃskāra pushes itself forward into awareness, try to follow it back to a locus, or energetic space, where it can be worked with. This is similar to how an energy healer will create a locus, or image, of a client when doing absence healing work with that client.

**3.** Find the cakras that feel as if they have the most affinity for the observed location of the saṃskāra. Cognitive components of an impression will usually have ājñā cakra as a primary relationship. Emotional components of an impression are often related to cakras below ājñā cakra.

**4.** After using one of the methods previously described in this book to balance the right and left energies at ājñā cakra, establish a relationship between the location of the saṃskāra and the internal junction of iḍā, piṅgalā and suṣumṇa (internal central location within the skull).

**5.** During exhalation, follow the lateral flow of energy from the center point of ājñā cakra through the location of the impression. During inhalation draw the energy back through the impression into the central region of ājñā cakra. The mantra "soḥaṃ" is useful for this practice. Merge the vibration of the sounds of the mantra "soḥaṃ" with the flow of prāṇa.

**6.** The affective component of a saṃskāra may have an affinity to cakras other than ājñā cakra. While clearing the energy flow through the saṃskāra in relation to ājñā cakra, the relationship of the impression to other cakras may become more apparent. If this is noticed, use the lateral flow associated with the breath and the mantra "soḥaṃ" to clear the energy flow in relation to the associated cakras while attending to the feeling component of the impression, wherever it may be located.

**7.** Similarly work with any bodily sensations that may be associated with the impression. Connect the sensations to the related cakras, and then clear the flow through the location of those sensations.

**8.** Perform the practices of steps four through seven simultaneously, sensing the flows related to the saṃskāra from more than one cakra at the same time. For many, this will be a challenge to their ability to remain focused.

**9.** Work with the saṃskāra is finished when there is a sense of peace, stillness, and/or nonattachment regarding the saṃskāra.

For those yoga practitioners who may have impressions resulting from severe trauma in their lives, one may wish to do this practice in the presence of a trusted therapist.

Flashbacks, and/or dissociation, may result when accessing one's particularly traumatic saṃskāras, especially if the practitioner has a history of posttraumatic stress disorder and/or dissociation.

***Something to Consider:***

Think about the mind's impressions being similar to a bucket of mud. One way to clean the bucket is to scoop up the mud and then scrub the sides of the bucket. One is then left with an empty bucket.

Another way to clear the bucket is to pour in a continuous stream of clear water, gently floating out the mud. Bringing the focus of the mind to stillness and bliss on a regular basis sets up impressions in the mind connected to the energy of that stillness and bliss. The stillness and bliss become the stream of clear water cleaning the bucket. The energy connected to the bliss radiates everywhere just as the energy of all impressions radiates everywhere. One is then left with a mind-filled bucket without the slightest ripple. It is easier to make a mind filled with stillness and bliss a tool of consciousness than it is to make a mind filled with mud a tool of consciousness.

# Transmutation and Transformation

In the previous chapters we have looked at gaining familiarity with subtleties of each of the cakras. We have also looked at the nature of saṃskāras and the relationship to the mind. Practices of transmutation and transformation require familiarity with textures of the elements associated with each cakra.

Sanskrit is a language of subtle vibrations. Consonants represent the potential to become something. That potential is activated or energized by the vowels. The textures of the elements earth, water, fire, and air are related to the following bīja mantras.

Lam = **L + am**, pronounced "lum" as in "lump". The texture is the vibration created by a lump of sand or earth dropping to the ground. The thud of the vibration creates the sound of the mantra "lam". It is the bīja mantra for mūlādhāra cakra.

Vam = **V + am**, pronounced "vwum" where the "V" has a vibration resembling a buzzing "W" as in the word "vodka". The texture of the water element is the vibration created by an ocean breaker as it rumbles onto the beach. Water is the element associated with svādiṣṭhāna cakra.

Ram = **R + am**, pronounced "ram" where the "R", when activated, has a roll to it as in "whirring". The vibration of the element fire is the roaring blast as one opens the door on a blast furnace. The texture of fire can also be much less forceful as one begins to focus on the light and illumination provided by the fire. The vibration of the texture then becomes less active and more peaceful, less rajasik and more sattvik. Fire is the element associated with maṇipūra cakra.

Yam = **Y + am**, pronounced "yum" as in "yummy". The vibration of the consonant "y" activated by the vowels "a" and "m" is a vibration of a wind or breeze passing through a narrow space. If one whispers this bīja mantra "yam", one can get a sense of the subtlety of the vibration of air or wind. Air is the element associated with anāhata cakra.

Bīja mantras for the remaining cakras are as follows:

"Ham", pronounced like "hum", is the seed mantra for viśuddha cakra. "Ham" is actually made up of three vowels and semi-vowels, namely an aspirated "H", or "ḥ", "a" that when elongated becomes "āāā", and "m" that when elongated becomes "ṃṃṃ". Each of the three sounds, when elongated, become three individual mantras, each of whose effect can be to lead the mind to silence. Silence is an absence of vibration or texture and is the element "ākāśa" associated with viśuddha cakra. When the sounds are sequenced together as the mantra "Ham" one translation is "That", meaning "all that is". This is because the silence (absence of vibration) of ākāśa has the capacity to accept any vibration and become anything.

"Soham", which has the vibratory characteristic of "soḥaṃ" (translated as I am That, where "That" is the totality of absolutely everything), is considered the seed mantra of ājñā cakra. The mind is considered to contain all the vibrations of the universe as conscious or unconscious saṃskāras. Ājñā cakra is considered to be the principle seat of that aspect of mind which contains the storehouse of saṃskāras (citta vṛtti).

Sahasrāra cakra has the seed mantra "Hamsa" (translated That I am), of which "soham" or "soḤaṃ" is considered to be a derivative. Sahasrāra cakra is related to saundarya lahari, which is made up of the potential for all that is and is possible.

### *The Practice of Bhūtaśuddhi*

The usual translation of bhūtaśuddhi is "purification of the elements" where "bhūta" is translated as "element" and "śuddhi" is translated as "purify". My teacher gave a different translation. "Bhūta" can also be translated as "past". He translated bhūtaśuddhi to mean "past purify". If we consider that we are made up as a constellation of vibrations of our past, it makes sense to think of our transmutation and transformation as being a purification of those past vibrations.

The practice of bhūtaśuddhi is generally done in a seated position with an erect spine, allowing alignment of the major cakras. It is helpful to have a working familiarity with the subtleties of the major cakras before attempting this practice.

**1.** Spend some time balancing the energies of iḍā and piṅgalā.

**2.** Bring one's awareness to the area between the ischial tuberosities within the region of mūlādhāra cakra. Balance the lateral flows of prāṇa and become aware of the texture of the element earth.

If the center point of mūlādhāra cakra is well lit, a mantra is sometimes infused with the gateway to help open the gateway to the central path of Śakti. This mantra is a single repetition of "hum" (English pronunciation “hoom” as in “whom”). Use of the mantra at this point can initiate the practice of bhūtaśuddhi.

Intone the vibration of each of the sounds of the bīja mantra “lam” into the earth element. The vibration and the earth may begin to move with the lateral flow of the prāṇas in all directions. When this has occurred for a few breaths, pull the vibration and the earth element into the centermost thread of suṣumṇa during an inhalation through the center point of mūlādhāra cakra. This will merge the activated earth element with the energy of Śakti.

**3.** With that final inhalation of step two, bring the awareness up the central channel to svādiṣṭhāna cakra. Become aware of the globe of water in the pelvic bowl and begin to intone the vibrations of the seed mantra “vam” with the water element as the water begins to surge and flow gently side-to-side. When the water infused with the mantra begins to uniformly move side-to-side, draw the activated water element into the central thread of Śakti through the center point at the base of the bowl which supports the globe of water.

**4.** During the final inhalation of step three, draw the awareness up the central channel to maṇipūra cakra. Balance the lateral flow of prāṇa through the 10 embers (or petals) of maṇipūra cakra, timing the flows with the breath. Intone the sounds of the bīja mantra “ram” into the flow, merging the vibrations with the fire and the light. When the activated fire element feels uniform in all directions, draw that activated fire element while inhaling into the central thread of Śakti through the center point at the base of the flame associated with maṇipūra cakra.

**5.** With the final inhalation of step four, draw the awareness up the central channel to anāhata cakra. Become aware of the central smoke, mist or fog present at the intersection of the triangles of anāhata cakra. Intone the vibration of the sounds of the bīja mantra "yam" with the air element present in that smoke, mist or fog. As the center point of light appears within that activated grayish mixture of air, inhale that activated air through the point of light into the central thread of Śakti.

**6.** During the final inhalation of step five, bring one's awareness to viśuddha cakra. The area of focus within which to intone a sound of the bīja mantra "Ham" is just behind the upper sternum in an area called kūrma nādī. The texture of this area is absolute stillness, the texture of ākāśa. Some may practice with all three sounds of the bīja mantra. However, intoning just one of the three sounds into the area of kūrma nādī can lead the mind to stillness. Finding which of the three sounds the mind prefers (as in the practice in the viśuddha cakra chapter) can be helpful for this step of bhūtaśuddhi. When the texture of stillness is apparent, pull the element of ākāśa into the central thread of Śakti during an inhalation.

**7.** During the final inhalation of step six, bring the awareness to the central area of ājñā cakra. Exhale the prāṇa through all the saṃskāras of the mind and inhale back through the saṃskāras to the central area of the cakra where iḍā, piṅgalā and suṣumṇa join deep within the skull. Intone the mantra "soḥaṃ" into the flow of prāṇa. "So" is timed with the inhale, and "Ḥaṃ" is timed with the exhale. When the activated flow feels uniform in all directions, inhale through all the saṃskāras through the junction of iḍā, piṅgalā, and suṣumṇa into the central thread of Śakti.

**8.** With the final inhalation of step seven, bring the awareness upward to the light under the vertex of the skull, the central illumination of the petals of sahasrāra cakra. Intone the mantra "Hamsa" to activate this region of potentials.

**9.** Bring the awareness of the activated elements back to the region of the heart cakra for these next two steps. Become aware of all the impurities in your entire being. Activate iḍā by either closing off the right nostril with the right thumb, through conscious manipulation of the prāṇa balance between iḍā and piṅgalā, or by slightly rotating the head a few degrees to the right without changing the alignment of the major cakras. Inhale the impurities into the region of the heart cakra. During this inhalation as well as during retention (kumbhaka), intone the vibration of the bīja mantra "yam" and the texture of air into the area of the impurities. Continue intoning the mantra as one then exhales remaining impurities through the right nostril with piṅgalā activated (with left nostril closure, conscious manipulation of the prāṇas, or slight head rotation to the left). This step is generally performed only for one breath, including the retention, though some prefer to perform the step for more than one breath.

**10.** With piṅgalā activated during inhalation, draw the element agni into the region of anāhata cakra to illuminate and/or incinerate any remaining impurities. Intone the bīja mantra "ram" into the region during inhalation, retention, and exhalation through the left nostril (with iḍā activated during exhalation). The illuminated and/or incinerated impurities follow the breath out the left nostril on exhalation. Some will draw the agni for this step from the solar fire at maṇipūra cakra or from the sun.

**11.** With iḍā activated, inhale and intone the bīja mantra "vam" into the region of sahasrāra cakra where soma cakra is located. During the retention and also during the exhalation (with piṅgalā activated), enjoy the sprinkle of the prāṇas collected there during the practice. These purified energies go to occupy the regions of previous impurities, transmuting and transforming with the help of overwhelming love and compassion (Śakti) that which was out of balance into that which is in balance.

**12.** Intone the vibration of the mantra "Hamsa" into the region of sahasrāra cakra timing "Ham" with one phase of the breath (inhalation or exhalation) and "sa" with the other phase of the breath.

**13.** One then begins the process of successively exhaling downward, beginning with the region of ājñā cakra. Exhale the quiescent saṃskāras in all directions to their appropriate locations while intoning the vibration of the mantra "soḥaṃ".

**14.** Exhale down to each successive cakra, intoning the vibration of the appropriate bīja mantra for each cakra as one releases each purified element into the region of the appropriate cakra.

## The Nature of Siddhis

While practicing the path of samāyā tantra, one may become aware of siddhis. "Siddhi" is generally translated as "accomplishment". An example of a siddhi would be the ability to levitate, to be able to add the quality of lightness to that space occupied by the body. The yoga sūtras mention siddhis as being related to a student's preparation and practice. There are, however, some individuals who exhibit such abilities without having followed the path of yoga in this life.

To understand how such abilities as siddhis might be possible, it is helpful to understand the nature of the universe from the viewpoint of yoga philosophy. As noted previously in this text, the nature of the universe is vibratory. The manifest universe consists of points which have accepted a vibration that results from an admixture of textures of the elements (bhūtas). Most of the universe, however, consists of points which have not yet accepted a vibration. These points appear silent, unmeasurable, and are a perfect balance of all the energies of the universe, hence appearing neutral, silent, without vibration. Because these points are unmeasurable, physicists in the past have considered them to be representative of empty space. More recent theories of physics, however, consider these points to be of infinite or nearly infinite energy density. If such a point accepts a vibration, it can manifest into anything. Even so-called "particles" of atoms contain many unmanifest points. In yoga these unmanifest points are called ākāśa, or ether, rather than empty space. This element, ākāśa, is perhaps related to what physicists call dark matter, that large portion of the universe (80% or more by some estimates) which physicists are unable to observe or measure and which is interspersed with that which is observable.

Vibratory nature of the universe means that the universe reabsorbs itself into a cloudy, undifferentiated state and from which it re-emerges many times per second. Like the refresh rate on a computer screen or television screen, this refresh rate is not noticed by ordinary senses. What re-emerges is generally consistent with what is expected according to natural laws with time as a constant. If natural laws were the only factors determining what would re-emerge, the future of the universe would be predictable with certainty. As a result, siddhis that do not conform to natural laws would not be possible.

For something observed not to conform to what is expected by the apparent natural laws related to time, space, and causation, there must be a way to transcend those laws. The practice of saṃyama allows the yogi or yogini to transcend those laws. Saṃyama is the simultaneous application of dhāraṇā (one's perfect concentration or focus), dhyāna (sustained focus on a single content of mind unbroken over time), and samādhi (an expanded state of conscious awareness) applied to a single content of mind.

The first step to transmuting or transforming a portion of the universe in a way that does not conform to natural law is to define the space within which one will focus. After observing what is currently there, one focuses on the desired result of the change needed, the mixture of textures of the elements the practitioner desires to replace what is currently present within the space. Such focus on that desired single content of mind must be held consciously and continuously even through the cloudy moments between reabsorption and re-emergence of the universe. The expansion of awareness called samādhi and the engagement of Śakti allows one's consciousness to transcend the vibratory nature of the universe.

### *Something to Consider:*

Like the mind, siddhis can become a distraction and an obstacle on the path of yoga. Also, like the mind, siddhis can be tools for fulfilling one's purpose and responsibilities in life. Non-attachment to siddhis that may have appeared during the course of one's practice is a useful attitude if one wishes to achieve knowledge of the union of self with Self.

# Clearing the Path for Śakti

Before mobilizing and working directly with the force of Śakti, it is advisable to prepare the pathways through which that energy will travel. In the preceding chapters are methods for becoming familiar with the major cakras. In this chapter we will look at the potential restrictions in flow that prevent Śakti from ascending through the energetic pathways.

Three restrictions must be addressed before the energy of Śakti can mobilize and ascend through the central channel of suṣumṇa. The gateway must be opened between mūlādhāra and svādiṣṭhāna cakras. The second restriction to flow is between maṇipūra and anāhata cakras. The third restriction is between the internal junction of ājñā cakra (the union of iḍā, piṅgalā, and suṣumṇa in the center of the skull) and sahasrāra cakra.

The first and second restrictions can be partially addressed with the hatha yoga practices of aśvini mudrā and nauli. The path from anāhata cakra and above will be addressed in the next chapter.

## *Aśvini Mudrā*

Before attempting aśvini mudrā, it is helpful to become familiar with the region of the pelvic floor. While standing on the mat as pictured, attempt to abduct the lower extremities. The feet will stick to the mat and the sit bones (ischial tuberosities) will move laterally, increasing the distance between them. The area of focus when working with aśvini mudrā is initially in the region between the ischial tuberosities. Support with hands above the knees in a standing position with knees slightly bent. Spread the sit bones slightly and gently contract the muscles at the opening of the anus. After the initial contraction at the opening of the anus, exhale and gently draw the pelvic floor muscles as well as the anus upward and inward during exhalation. Becoming familiar with and progressing in this practice, will lead one to feel the tissues near the ischial tuberosities being pulled around those sit bones and inwardly. Then one can slowly relax the tissues with a smooth inhalation.

If additional support is needed, one can place the buttocks against a wall. Once learned, the pelvic floor techniques can be practiced in any symmetric position.

### *Preparation for Nauli Kriya*

The word "nauli" is derived from two Sanskrit words. *"Nala"* is sometimes translated as "boat", but in this context can be translated as "a string" or as "a tubular vessel" (the chain of rectus abdominis muscles that protrude on one side as one performs nauli). The second word "lola" translates as "to roll" or "churning".

There is a sequential set of preliminary practices that are helpful if one chooses to learn nauli. Contraindications for these practices include active inflammation of any kind in the abdomen, including disorders of intestinal inflammation, endometriosis, or menstruation. These practices should also not be performed during pregnancy. Mesh repairs of the pelvic floor, abdominal wall or inguinal hernia mesh repairs are also contraindications for nauli as well as some of the preliminary practices. When in doubt, consult your health care practitioner.

The following series of self-applied neuromuscular techniques can be beneficial when working with fascial restrictions that can interfere with the performance of nauli. Divide the area between the rib cage and the pelvis into three sections as pictured.

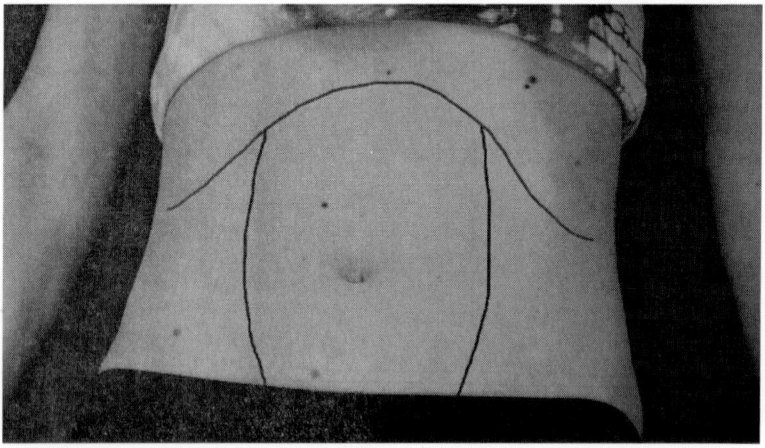

*Abdominal Release Series*

**Position:** Lie on the back with knees up and feet shoulder width apart. Contraindications include abdominal and inguinal hernia mesh repairs, some pelvic floor mesh repairs, any active inflammation (including menstruation), pregnancy, and current hernias.

**Skin Rolling:** Lift the tissue between thumb and fingers on one side (outer or lateral third) below the ribs. Keep the tissue lifted as you roll the tissue between thumbs and fingers, progressing from below the ribs downward to the pelvis. Repeat two to three times on each side.

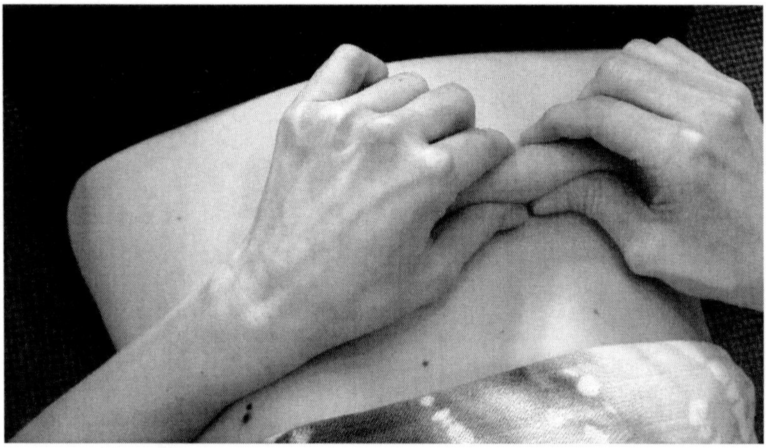

**Lift and Twist**: Lift the tissue somewhat more on one side, twist and hold for 5-15 seconds while doing deep diaphragmatic breathing, then release.

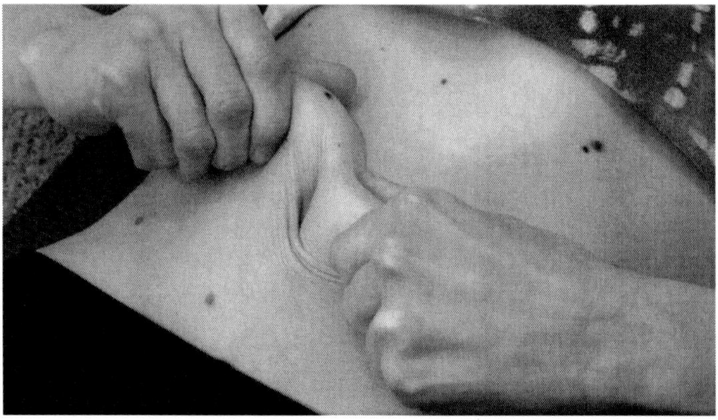

If you have weakness of the central ligament of the abdomen, grasp the tissue on each side and move the hands toward each other to support the central ligament before lifting and twisting one side. Do this on each side at the level of the navel, above the level of the navel below the ribs, and in the lower abdomen below the level of the navel.

**Rectus Abdominus Stretch:** Clasp the hands and use the heels of hands to scoop under the navel and raise the rectus abdominus muscles upward. Hold for 5-15 seconds while doing deep diaphragmatic breathing, then release. Repeat the technique below the navel and again above the navel.

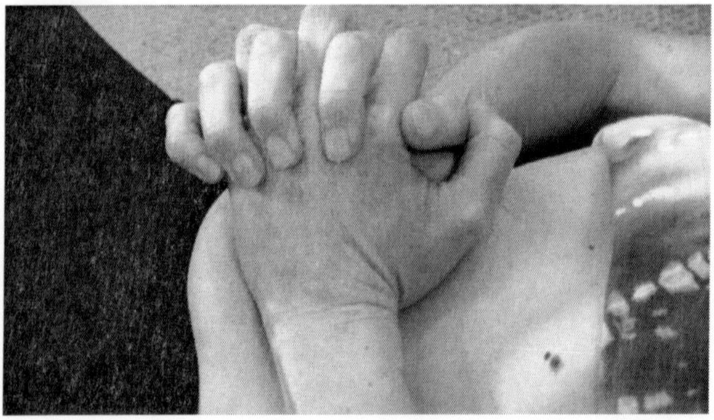

Alternatively, one can reach behind the rectus abdominus muscles with the fingers and keep the thumbs on the anterior surface of the abdomen.

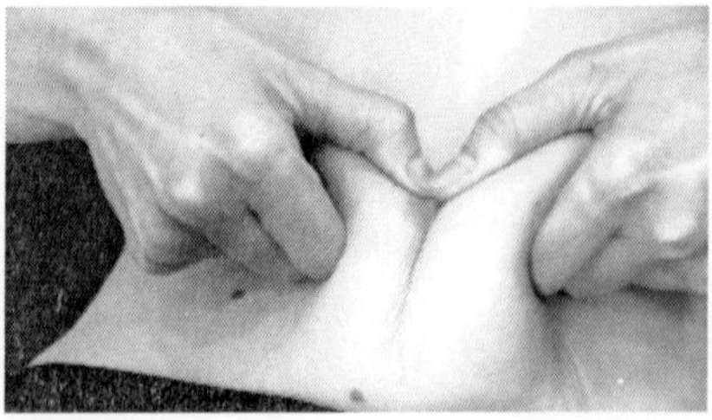

### *Differential Control of Abdominal Musculature*

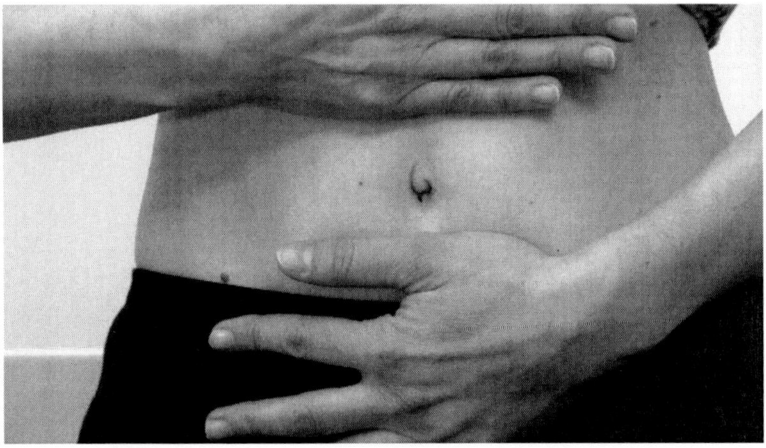

In a seated posture with an erect spine, place one hand on the abdomen below the navel and one hand above the navel. Exhale first below the navel, then above the navel. Inhale first above the navel, then below the navel. To further refine abdominal control, one can pull in above the pubic bone at the beginning of exhalation. Then pull in just below the navel, then just above the navel, and finally just below the ribcage. This sequentially involves contracting the four pairs of rectus abdominus muscles from below upward. The sequence is then reversed from above downward during an inhalation.

### *Ujjayi Breath*

The following form of ujjayi breath helps prepare the practitioner for the practice of uḍḍīyana, the stomach lift necessary to perform nauli. To properly perform this practice, it is helpful to prepare the secondary muscles of breathing that help to expand the rib cage as well as lift the clavicles and first ribs. The following series is offered as one way to help prepare for ujjayi breath.

### *Preparing Accessory Breathing Muscles*

If you're not familiar with the anatomy of the neck and the first ribs, please perform an online search for these structures and study the anatomy before performing this series. Please practice gently and be comfortable with each practice in the series.

**1.** Either supine or standing, reach a thumb under the upper ridge of the trapezius muscle. While grasping the outer aspect with the fingers, work the muscle with the thumb, pressing the ridge of the muscle against the fingers. Work the border from the shoulder to the base of the skull. Repeat on the opposite side.

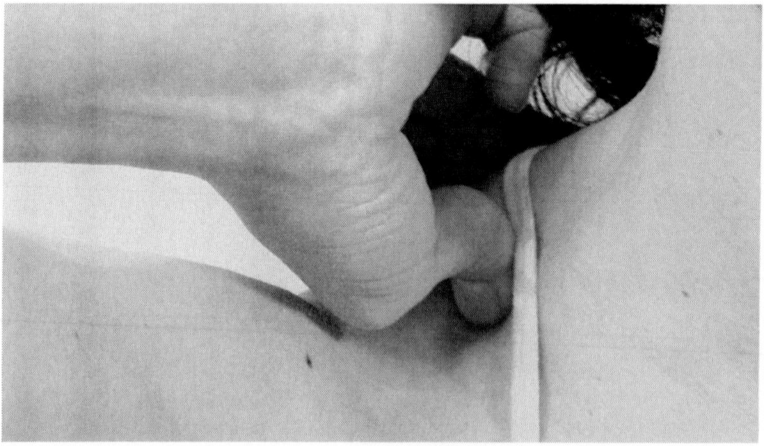

**2**. Find the prominences of the transverse processes of the cervical vertebrae just below the skull below the ear. Stay posterior to the transverse processes and massage from lateral to posterior between the ridge of the skull and the transverse process.

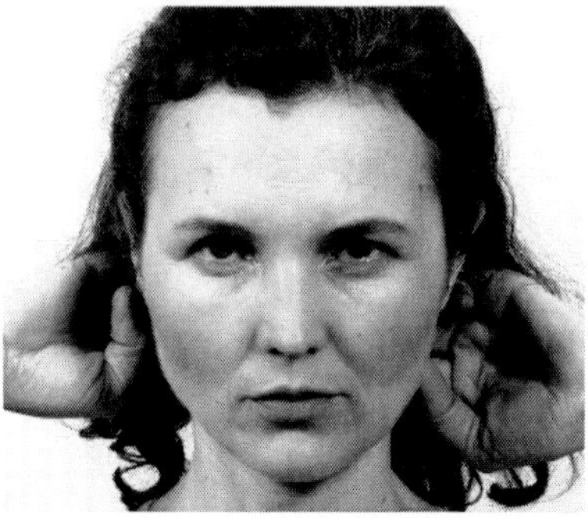

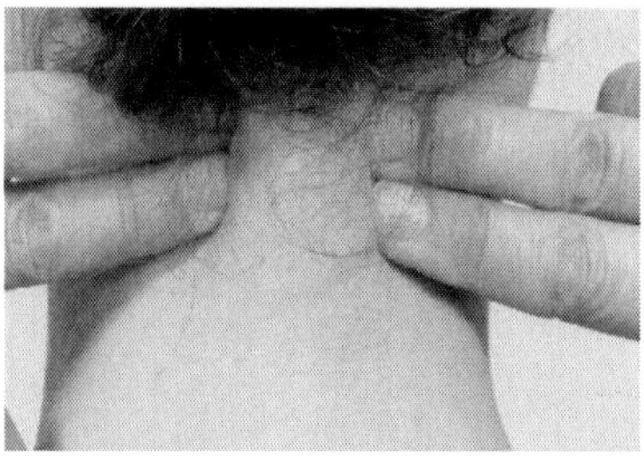

**3.** Cross-fiber from anterior to posterior between each pair of transverse processes of the cervical spine, staying behind (posterior to) the transverse processes. Cross-fiber means to stroke in one direction only (from lateral to medial in this case) and then release before stroking again.

**4.** To stretch the digastric muscles, place the thumbs inside the angle of the mandible (jaw bone) and stretch the tissue toward the chin, keeping the thumbs medial to the mandible.

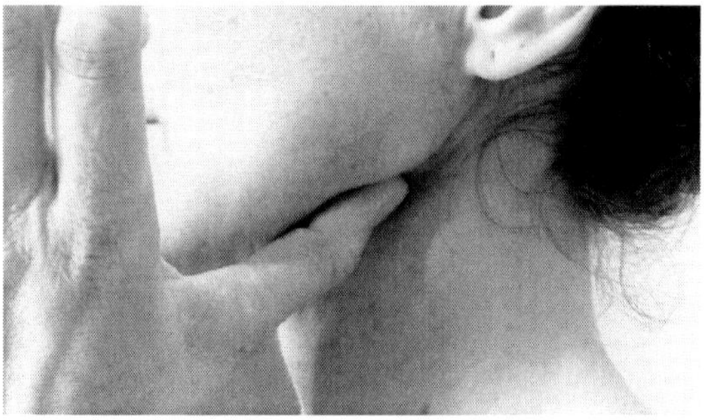

**5.** For the "Gumby" pose, pull the tissue covering the angle of the mandibles laterally, twist gently to engage, and then hold while gently moving the head. This helps release the muscles of the jaw and upper neck when performed properly. If you have temporomandibular (TMJ) joint issues, please consult with your TMJ specialist before performing this technique.

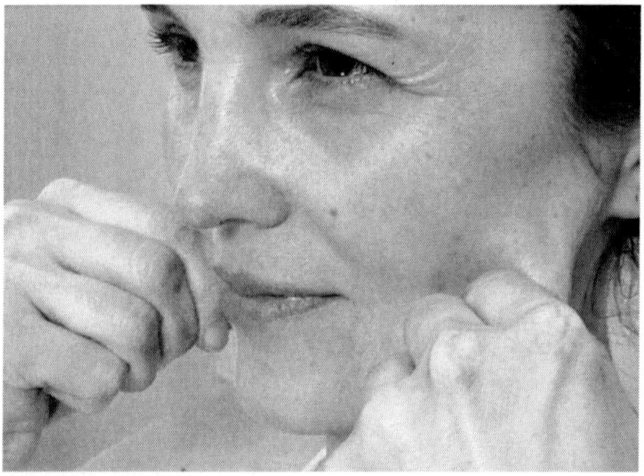

**6.** Compress the sternocleidomastoid muscles at various level. Be cautions with the distal portion near the collar bone, as the carotid bodies are located medial and deep to this muscle and may trigger changes in blood pressure.

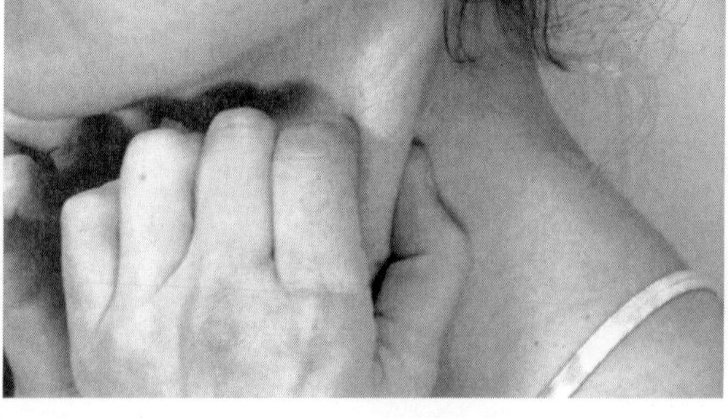

**7.** To free up the junction between the second rib and sternum, place the thumbs on the second ribs (the ribs immediately below the collar bones) and gently alternately press posteriorly. This will help mobilize the tissues between the clavicles (collar bones) and the second ribs just below the collar bone. Keep in mind first ribs are primarily in the neck.

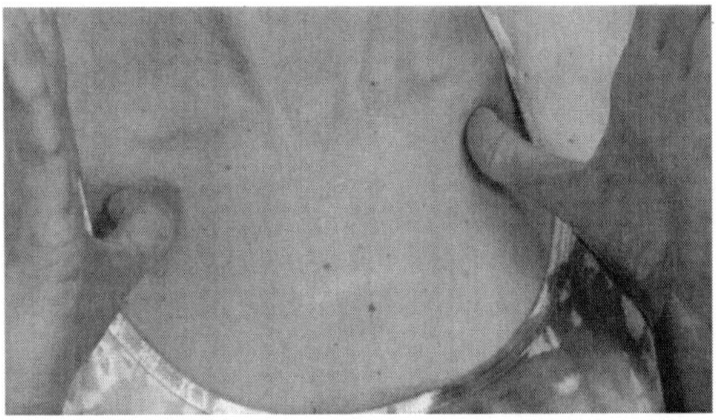

**8.** One technique to free up the first rib is as follows:

a. Place the hands on the hips. Then raise one shoulder and move it anteriorly.

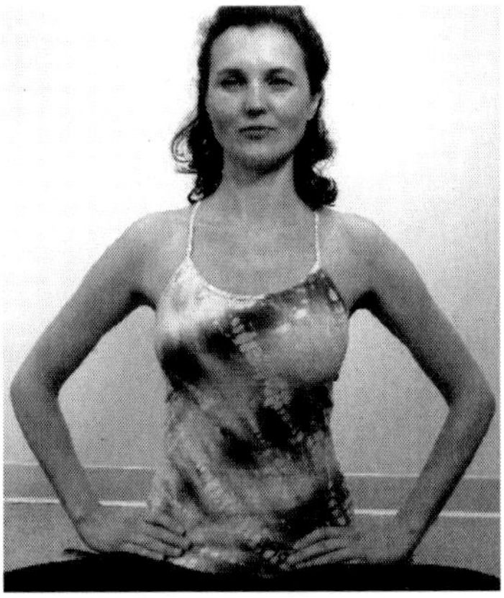

b. Keeping the chin parallel to the ground, gently rotate the head toward the raised shoulder. If the neck does not rotate comfortably or you have been advised not to rotate the neck because of medical conditions such as severe osteoporosis, please do not attempt this technique.

c. With the chin parallel to the ground, move the head towards the raised shoulder. Alternate this movement with moving the back of the head towards the opposite shoulder. Do not raise the chin while translating between the two positions.

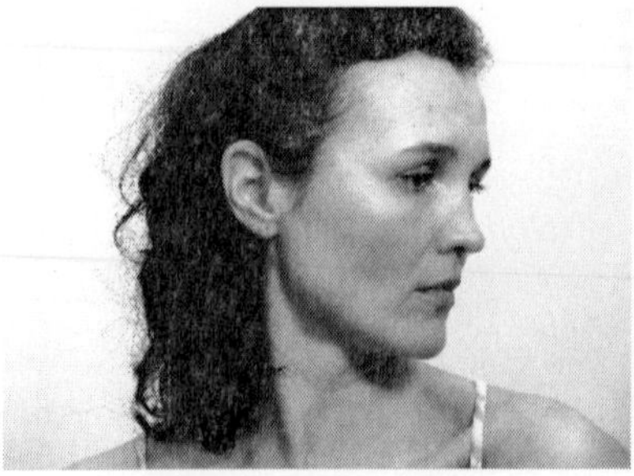

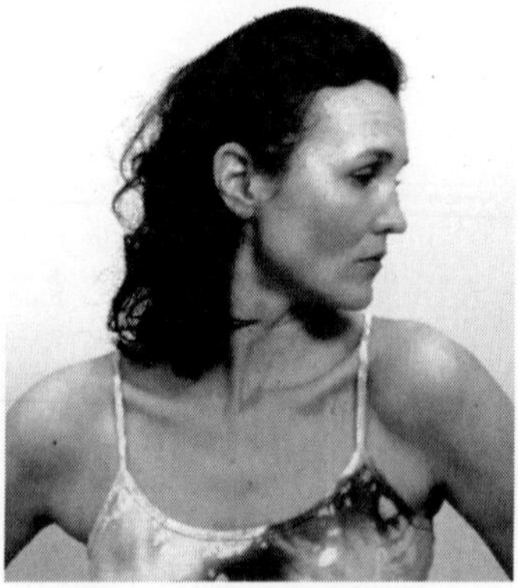

d. Perform the series to the opposite side.

**9.** Once the first rib has been mobilized, one is ready to work the lower portion of the anterior attachment of the sternocleidomastoid muscles.

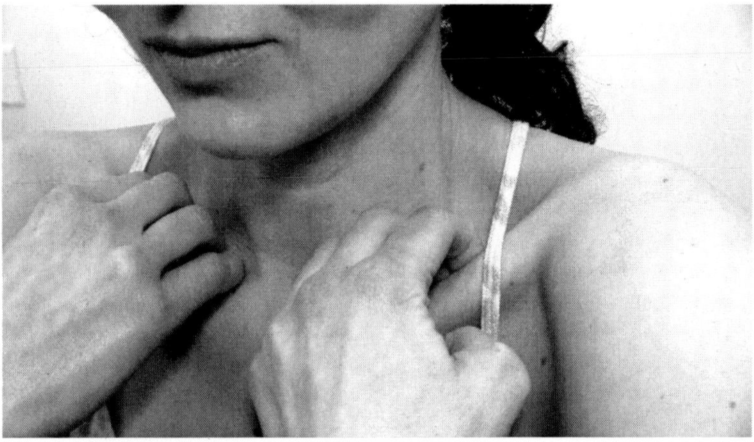

Bring both your shoulders forward and reach the fingers inside the clavicles. Cross-fiber toward the midline, paying particular attention to anterior sternocleidomastoid muscle attachments near the junction where the clavicles join the sternum. Stroke only towards the midline and then release. When performing self-applied cross-fiber techniques, the stroke is in one direction only, allowing the muscle to release before stroking again.

**10.** Free up the intercostal muscles between the ribs. These muscles criss-cross between each pair of ribs. The externally oriented muscles can expand the rib cage, and the internally oriented muscles can bring the ribs closer together. If you're not familiar with the anatomy, please find images of the intercostal muscles online, and study their anatomy and function.

a. Stand with your feet parallel and place your thumb or finger on the lowest ribs on each side of your thoracic cage.

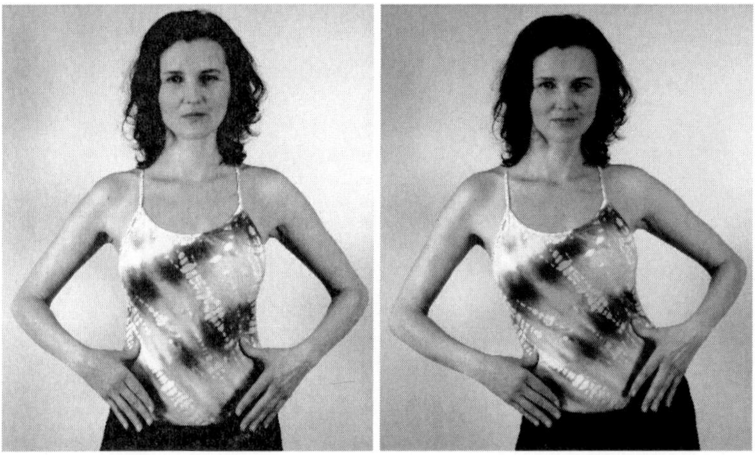

b. Translate the thoracic cage side to side. Observe whether there is some motion between each of the lowest ribs and the rib above each as you translate.

c. Next place your fingers or thumbs on each pair of ribs above the lowest ribs. While translating note the ease of movement between each rib pair and the ribs immediately above and below. If restriction is noted between any pairs of ribs one can try the following self-applied techniques to increase the mobility. These techniques should not be practiced by people who already have hyper mobile ribs, cartilage detachments or other rib issues without first consulting with their healthcare practitioner.

i. Use the thumbs or fingers to cross-fiber the intercostal muscles between restricted ribs. One can simply follow the grooves between the ribs as far as one can reach posteriorly.

ii. Alternately one can place a thumb or finger to stabilize the restriction, and then gently move the thoracic cage around the area of restriction until it frees up. The following two pictures illustrate this.

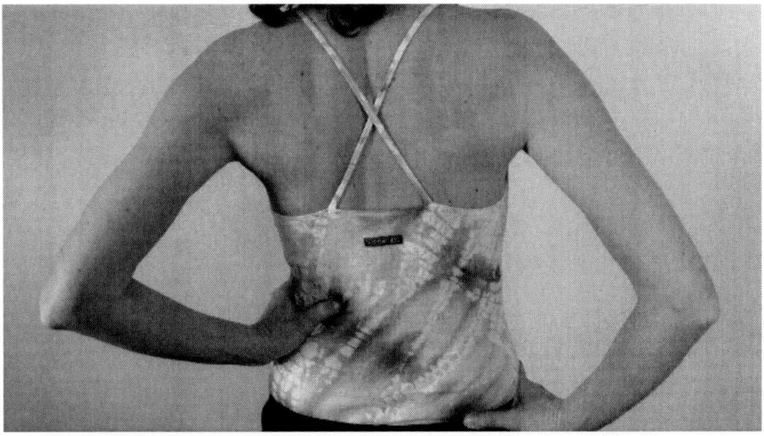

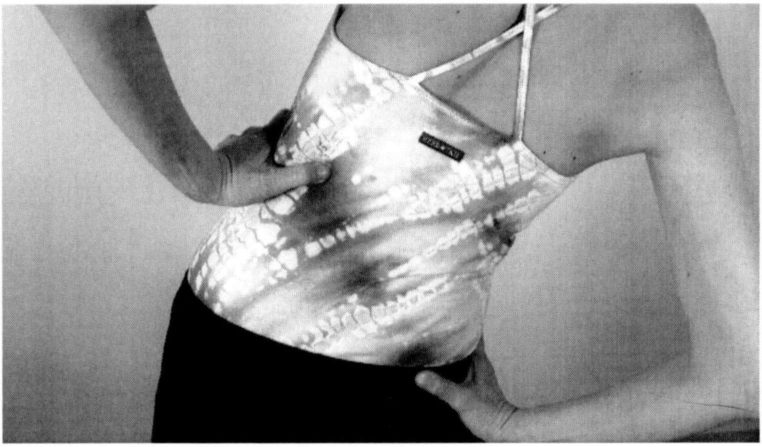

A more general technique for mobilizing the rib cage:

**1.** Stand with feet parallel and more than shoulder width apart.

**2.** Clasp the hands behind and extend the elbows. This will bring the arms away from the torso and mobilize the shoulder blades.

**3.** Keeping the arms away from the torso, perform a gentle torso twist. There should be near minimal movement of the pelvis for this rib mobilization.

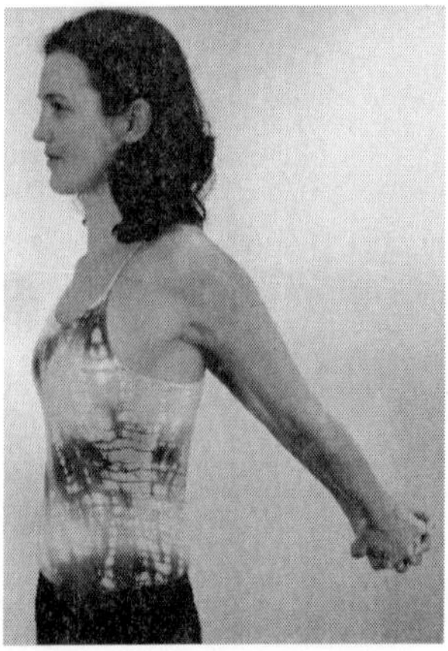

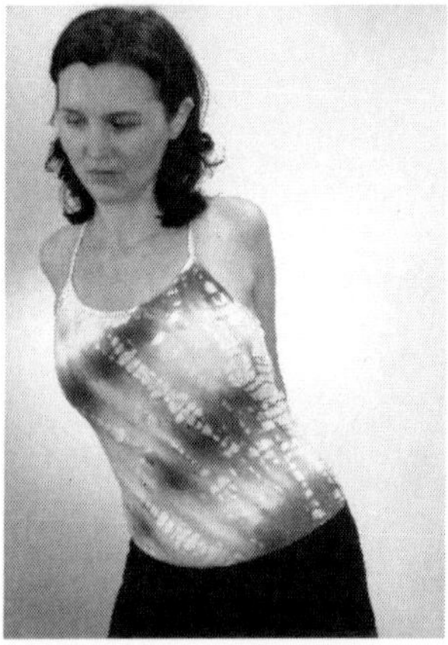

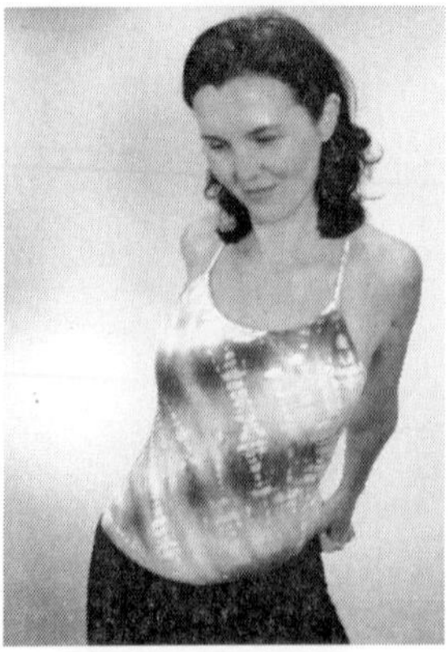

Once the preparation of the accesory muscles of breathing is complete, one is then ready to practice ujjayi breath.

### *Ujjayi: A Chest Breath*

In a seated posture with straight spine, exhale while drawing the abdomen toward the spine. Once drawn inward, the abdominal muscles below the navel do not release. Energetically, this serves to restrict the upward flow of prāṇa below the navel during inhalation. As a result of that partial restriction, the lateral flow through the solar fire is increased. This recruits the vitality of agni to help clear and smooth the prāṇa flow within the central channel.

Inhale by expanding the chest with the accessory muscles of breathing while the lower abdomen remains drawn inward. Partially close the glottis and begin a gentle constriction of the vocal cords to create a soft sound with both inhalation and exhalation. As the sound is produced, the left and right channels of flow are partially restricted, increasing the flow through the central channel. If the glottis becomes dry, perform a version of khecharī mudrā until saliva forms and the glottis is moistened.

### *Khecarī Mudrā*

Curl the tongue back to contact the soft palate behind the hard palate that is the roof of the mouth. Full khecarī mudrā brings the tongue into the nasal cavity from the throat but requires elongation of the tongue. This simpler version is enough to moisten the glottis.

*Kapālabhāti*

One increases the rate of exhalation using the abdominal muscles below as well as above the navel. Inhalation is relaxed and slower. One must focus to use the muscles between the pubic bone and the navel, as these are often neglected in breath practice. Start slowly by performing just a few breaths in the beginning to avoid hyperventilation. Then gradually build up the repetitions. Make transitions between phases of the breath as smooth as they were while performing diaphragmatic breathing. Smooth transitions are as essential to influencing energetic patterns during accelerated breathing as they are during diaphragmatic breathing.

*Variations of kapālabhāti*

a) One alternate nostril pattern has two breaths exhaled through each nostril in multiples of four-breath cycles (two breaths each nostril).

b) Another four-breath cycle involves performing one breath through one nostril facing forward and next breath with head turned to the side of the open nostril. Then one switches nostrils and performs one breath forward through the open nostril. The fourth breath is performed through that nostril after turning the head again to the side of the open nostril. The following four pictures illustrate the positions for this four-breath cycle.

1. 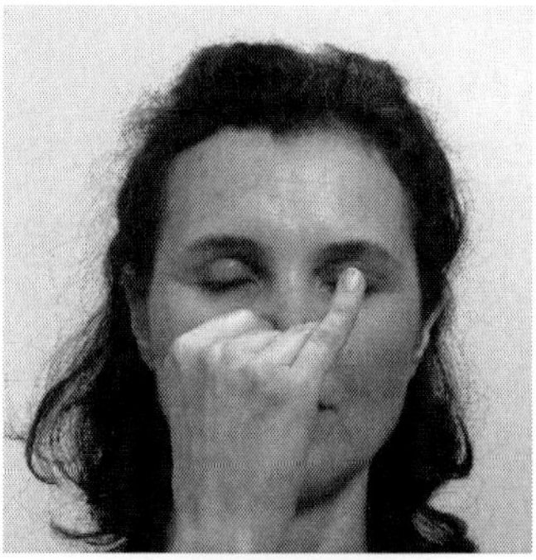

2. 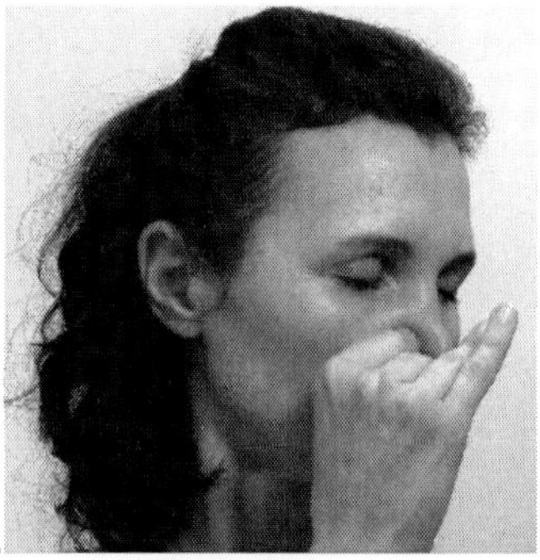

3. 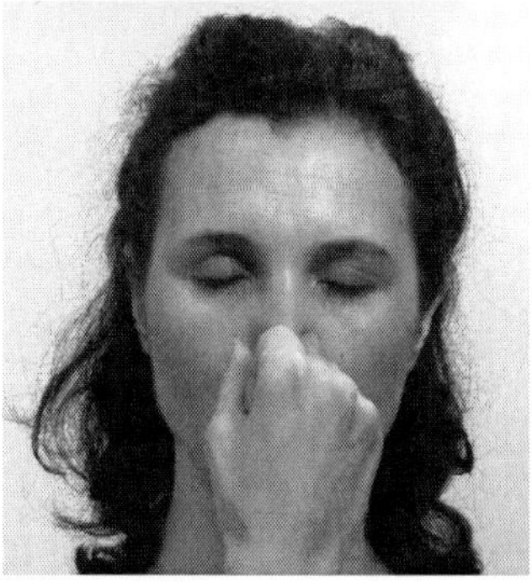

4. 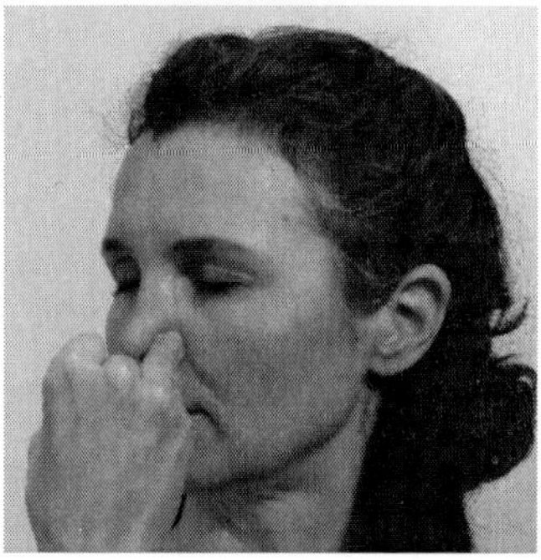

### *Bhastrika*

This technique involves accelerated exhalation using muscles above and below the navel on exhalation and accelerated contraction of the diaphragm muscle on inhalation. Begin with an exhalation and finish with a full inhalation regardless of number of breaths performed. Transitions between phases of the breath are smooth without pauses. When operating a bellows in a blacksmith shop or while playing a harmonium, one does not break the bellows with forceful contractions. Let the belly dance with the breath with full control, including smooth transitions without the slightest pause. When performing bhastrika or kapālabhāti, you may wish to protect the perineum with a small cushion between the ischial tuberosities or by engaging the pelvic floor muscles.

### *Stomach Lift (Uḍḍīyana)*

It is helpful to practice ujjayi, kapālabhāti, and bhastrika prior to practicing uḍḍīyana. The increased oxygenation of tissues will be helpful in assisting the practitioner to remain comfortable during the retention (bahya kumbhaka) phase of uḍḍīyana.

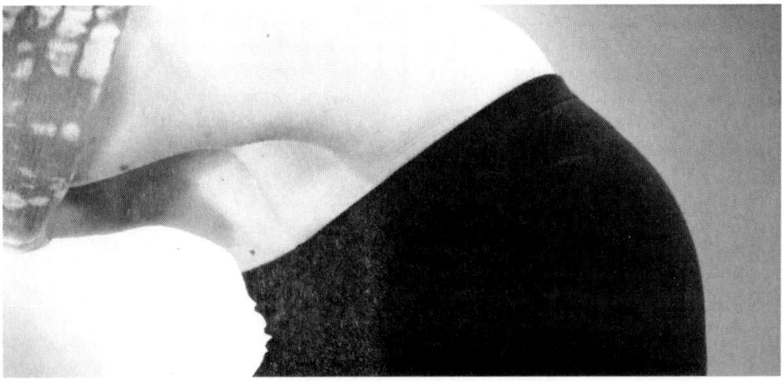

Exhale, drawing the navel toward the spine. Then retain the breath, preventing inhalation, and expand the chest to draw the abdominal contents upward. This chest expansion uses the same secondary muscles of breathing that were used to perform ujjayi breath. The abdominal musculature may initially assist in rolling the abdominal contents upward by gently contracting initially below the navel and then above the navel. Abdominal musculature and diaphragm then need to be relaxed for the abdominal contents to fully move upward under the lower ribs. Tuck the chin into the jugular notch above the sternum to establish the chin lock (jālandhara bandha). This will retain the breath after exhalation and can help prevent inhalation. When ready to inhale, slightly raise the chin and re-establish control of the abdominal musculature to allow a slow, controlled inhalation and release. For the practice of uḍḍīyana as well as the remaining practices in this section, it is helpful to place a mirror on the floor to observe the abdomen.

### *Differential Control of Rectus Abdominis Muscles*

Create the stomach lift. Then use motion of hips and sacrum on one side to press one side of rectus abdominus musculature outward while breath is retained after exhalation. Pressing the hand into the thigh above the knee also helps to isolate and contract the rectus muscle on that same side. Reverse sides by pressing the opposite hip and rectus muscle forward while pressing the hand into the thigh just above the knee. These maneuvers are pictured as follows:

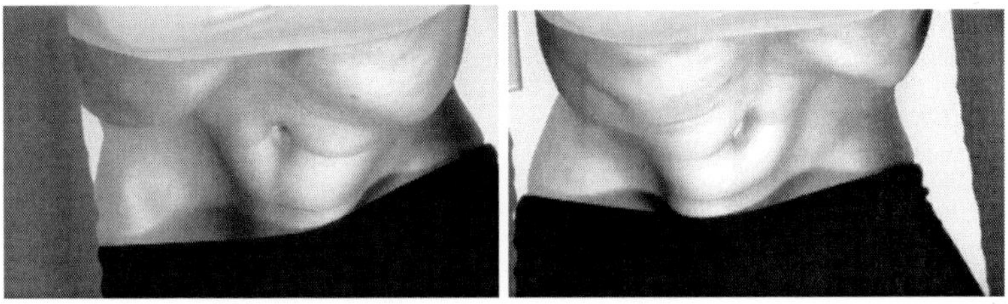

After control is learned with each side, then practice pressing both sides out at the same time.

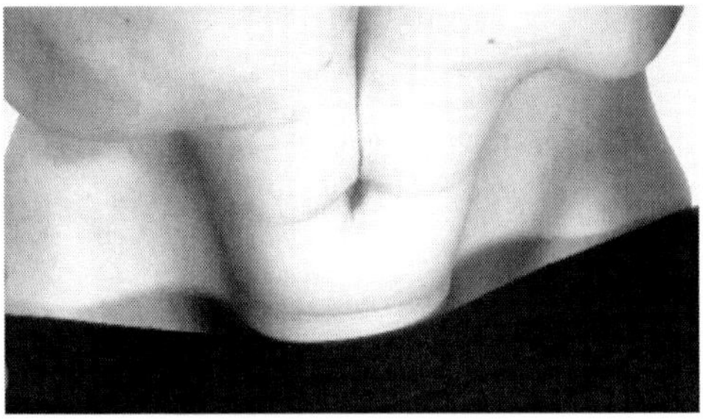

### *Agnisāra with Retention*

Sanskrit scholars differ regarding the definition of the term, agnisāra. Regarding the following practice, it appears to mean making use of the knowledge of the essence of the element, fire, to transmute or transform dullness into vitality on a physical and energetic level (annamaya and prāṇamaya kośas), as well as to illuminate ignorance and sharpen discernment (manomaya and vijñānamaya kośas). My teacher said that for the year he had confined himself in a cave where he could not completely stand, his hatha yoga practice consisted of agnisāra.

If one is not comfortable with retention, there are practices that can be performed to build and move the energies of the solar fire without retention. These will be presented following this section. Refrain from any practice with retention if it cannot be executed comfortably with steadiness of mind and body.

While exhaling and creating aśvini mudrā, exhale below the navel, then above the navel in order to help roll the abdominal contents up under the rib cage. Create the lift needed while retaining the breath at the end of exhalation by expanding the chest while holding the chin lock (jālandhara bandha) as in the practice of uḍḍīyana. When ready to release, slightly raise the chin allowing air to inhale slowly while gradually relaxing the secondary muscles of breathing in the chest and neck. Regain control of the abdominal musculature and begin inhaling with the upper abdomen and then the lower abdomen while releasing aśvini mudrā.

### *Variation of Agnisāra with Retention*

One can churn the abdominal contents upward and downward during retention to intensify the effect on the solar plexus. Attend to the shifts in energy flow as the navel moves anteriorly and posteriorly with this practice.

### *Ākuñcana Prasāraṇa (A & P Breath)*

One can think of ākuñcana prasāraṇa as resembling the performance of agnisāra without the retention. During exhalation, aśvini mudrā is performed while drawing the navel toward the spine. During inhalation, the diaphragm contracts as the belly expands and one releases aśvini mudrā.

While releasing aśvini mudrā, one might become aware of the prāṇa flow ascending from the area of mūlādhāra cakra. This energetic effect can also be noticed during the retention phase of agnisāra. If iḍā and piṅgalā are perfectly balanced during agnisāra, Śakti can be recruited through the opening of the lower gateway at mūlādhāra cakra. This leads to an effect commonly referred to as prāṇa bath.

### *Nauli*

Create the churning from left to right with combined alternate flexing of rectus abdominis muscles and slight hip motion after breath retention during uḍḍīyana. Left to right rotation assists the flow through the colon. Even if one rotates in both directions during the practice, it is best to finish by rotating left to right, following the natural track of the large intestine.

## Clearing the Path Above Anāhata Cakra

Two practices that help clear the prāṇa in the central channel are aum kriya and śītalī karaṇa. These practices help clear the energetic restrictions in flow within the central channel. Previously presented in this text were the practices of aśvini mudrā, agnisāra, and nauli which are also helpful in this regard, as the manipulation of the physical structures also have an energetic effect. Ujjayi breath, as presented in this text, helps to incorporate the fire element for energetic clearing of the upper central pathway.

### *Aum Kriya:*

One method to achieve pratyāhāra is Aum Kriya. After one has learned to sense the flows of prāṇa and apāna, one can practice the following method effectively. The practice is done in śavāsana. Remember that "śav" means corpse. A result of practicing aum kriya is to consciously experience the characteristics of a corpse, namely that of stillness and an absence of gross sensory perception.

While performing śavāsana, establish diaphragmatic breathing. Become aware of the flows of prāṇas ascending and descending in the more external central channel connecting the cakras. The more internal aspect of the central channel is suṣumnā nādī. Around this internal aspect are the flows of prāṇa and apāna, prāṇa flowing upward with inhalation, and apāna flowing downward with exhalation. Initially one can simply follow the flows upward and downward as far as consciousness wishes to go through the chain of cakras. This may simply be feeling the flow through one or two of the cakras, or it may involve all the major cakras. Consciousness may also wish to flow downward on the exhale through mūlādhāra cakra (root cakra). Rather than trying to follow the flow of prāṇa down the extremities, keep awareness on the central channel that extends downward between the knees, ankles, and feet. There is a nodal point of energy along that central channel between the knees as well as between the ankles and feet.

The mantra “Om” has three syllables “A”, “U”, and “M”. When practicing aum kriya it is important to make the transitions between the three syllables as smooth as possible. The practice of aum kriya involves the incorporating the vibration of the mantra “AUM” while focusing on the flows of prāṇa and apāna. Begin the practice after establishing diaphragmatic breathing and balancing the flow of breath in the right and left nostrils, bringing iḍā and piṅgalā as close to balance as possible. During inhalation, follow the energy inward to the internal junction of iḍā, piṅgalā and suṣumṇa. Follow the flow of breath from ājñā cakra (the internal junction of iḍā, piṅgalā and suṣumṇa near the pituitary gland at the center of the skull) to the light under the vertex (crown) of the skull, part of sahasrāra cakra. Then begin exhaling and following apāna from sahasrāra through the chain of cakra’s all the way down to a point between the ankles and feet. Let the mind focus internally on the sound “A” at sahasrāra, transitioning to “U” between ājñā and viśuddha cakras, and then transitioning to the sound “M” between viśuddha and anāhata cakras as one follows the flow of apāna downward. Exhalation should be at least the length of inhalation. Make the transitions between phases of the breath smooth. This also means making the transitions between the sounds of "M" and "A" smooth as well. Let the vibrations of the mantra follow the path rather than remaining as a cognitive repetition in the area of the skull.

During inhalation one follows the flow of prāṇa upward beginning with the sound "A" at the feet, transitioning to "U" as one approaches viśuddha cakra, and then transitioning to the sound "M" after passing viśuddha cakra and continuing up to the region of sahasrāra cakra. On both the upward and downward flow one transitions to the sound "U" while following the energy through the region of the throat cakra. Initially the breath may not feel long enough to exhale and reach between the feet. One can practice between the crown cakra and mūlādhāra cakra for a time with the breath ratio of 2:1 exhalation to inhalation before lengthening and extending the exhalation to reach between the feet. Sensing the prāṇas in this manner can lead to feelings of joy and lightness. After practicing this method for some time, one may get the sense that one is pulling energy in from the cosmos as one inhales. Extending the exhalation past mūlādhāra cakra and the feet may help accentuate that experience. If suṣumnā awareness is established during this practice, one can very quickly go to that silence where there is no longer input from the body's gross senses. This is a state of pratyāhāra. A guide may appear that will clarify why these practices are considered part of the path of fire and light. When one is ready to come out of the practice, exhalation is shortened again to a more normal breath ratio of 2:1 or less until one is feeling the flows only between ājñā cakra and sahasrāra cakra. The breath may be very fine and nearly imperceptible at that point.

A few cautions are necessary for this practice. When one comes out of the practice, it is important to do so gradually. When the body is in such a state of immobility and deep relaxation, tendons and ligaments can become strained if one suddenly moves when first coming out of the practice. For this reason, it is also important to pick a place and circumstance where one is not likely to be suddenly interrupted.

### *Śītalī Karaṇa:*

Śīthalī karaṇa is a practice to clear the prāṇa flow within the central channel between the cakras. In the chapter on svādiṣṭhāna cakra we experienced energy of the ascending and descending pathways related to cultivation of the energy of svādiṣṭhāna cakra. In contrast, śītalī karaṇa focuses on the relationship between the cakras and sahasrāra cakra.

This practice is performed in śavāsana. As during the practice of aum kriya, balance the energies of iḍā and piṅgalā. Find the center point of ājñā cakra where iḍā, piṅgalā, and suṣumṇa intersect at the center point within the skull. Inhale up to sahasrāra cakra and focus on the prāṇas in the following sequence:

**a.** While exhaling downward and inhaling upward, follow the prāṇas in the central channel between the enumerated sets of points for ten breaths between each pair of points.

**i.** Crown of the head and the midpoint between the toes.

**ii.** Crown of the head and the midpoint between the ankles.

**iii.** Crown of the head and the midpoint between the knees.

**b.** Next exhale downward and inhale upward five times each between the cakras.

**i.** Sahasrāra and mūlādhāra cakras.

**ii.** Sahasrāra and maṇipūra cakras.

**iii**. Sahasrāra and anāhata cakras.

**iv.** Sahasrāra and viśuddha cakras.

**v.** Sahasrāra and ājñā cakras.

**c.** Focus on the prāṇa flow between the two nostrils (between the indentation above the upper lip through the nose bridge to the projection of ājñā cakra between the eyebrows). As one exhales the prāṇa flow is downward and outward through that razor thin plane of energy that separates the right and left. The flow is upward and inward on the inhale. Do this for at least ten breaths.

**d.** Repeat step (b) in the reverse order of pairing, still exhaling downward and inhaling upward with the prāṇa flow. Some practitioners also include the pairing between svādhiṣṭhāna and sahasrāra cakras in steps (b) and (d).

**e.** Repeat step (a) in reverse order.

**f.** Some practitioners simply prefer to feel the prāṇa flows between each pair of cakras. This is done by holding the perception of each cakra of the pair in one's awareness, experiencing the resonance between each pair of cakras. This allows for the length of the breath to remain extended, even between those cakras that are close to each other such as ājñā cakra and sahasrāra cakra.

## Mastering Consciousness Quarter by Quarter

The *Māṇḍūkya* Upaniṣad states that one should know "AUM" quarter by quarter. Remaining consciously focused during all four states of awareness is one interpretation of that statement. The first sound of the mantra, "A", relates to waking state. The second sound, "U', relates to dream state. The third sound, "M", relates to deep sleep. The fourth sound of the mantra "AUM" is silence and relates to a state called turiya. Remaining consciously focused during the first three states and the transitions between those states can result in access and entry into that state called turiya.

Much of this text has focused on mastering the subtleties of conscious awareness and are practiced in waking state and meditation. Many people, especially children, are able to remain aware and consciously direct their dream state. The first step is to consciously realize that one is dreaming. Directing fantasies in waking state can be helpful to begin the process of developing awareness of one's dream state. Children often enjoy directing their fantasies as a normal part of their creative lives. Once one has gained the ability to recognize the dream state as a dream, then one can begin the practice of directing events and abilities during the dream. Mastering the ability to fly in one's dream, or to swim underwater while comfortably breathing water, for example, can help one learn to direct one's dreaming state.

One practical reason for mastering awareness during the dream state is that during conscious dreaming, teachers and guides may appear and interact with you in situations that may not be practically available during the waking state. My teacher said that whenever he appears in dream, it is not a dream.

Conscious or sleepless sleep as it is sometimes called can be more of a challenge. The following practice of yoga nidrā is offered:

### *Yoga Nidrā*

The practice of yoga nidrā presented here is taken, in large part, from my book Practical Yoga Sūtras.

There are many techniques taught in various traditions to lead the student toward the state of consciousness called yoga nidrā. Some common elements of many of these techniques are: 1) establish smoothness of breath; 2) try to establish free flow of prāṇa in all areas of the body; 3) clear the flow of prāṇa in the central channel; 4) balance the solar and lunar energies, the "ha" and the "tha"; 5) center the mind's tactile awareness in anāhata cakra while extending exhalation until it is twice as long as inhalation. Master these five steps without losing conscious awareness as the body goes into sleep state. This practice should be done with the final step lasting no more than ten minutes. The place of practice should be absolutely quiet with no chance of interruption as injury can occur if suddenly interrupted during this practice. The sense of sound can be particularly acute, and noise can damage the hearing mechanism.

The specific steps of yoga nidrā practice as originally taught to me are as follows:

1. Practice śavāsana with diaphragmatic breathing on a surface which allows for an erect spine. This practice should not be done in a soft bed such as a water bed or a recliner, as this would allow the spine to curve instead of remaining erect. It is important that the lower rib cage not compress the abdomen while breathing. The neck should be supported as the supporting structures of the neck can become lax and strained with prolonged practice of śavāsana.

### *61 Points as Part of Yoga Nidrā*

2. The preliminary practice is that of 61 points. This practice is used to survey the energy points and flows within the body. As the points are followed, establish a tactile awareness at each point. Rather than jumping from point-to-point, transition the awareness tactiley through the tissues. For example, when allowing awareness to move from the shoulder to the elbow, try to feel the tissues of the biceps, triceps, humerus, and associated tendons. Move through the upper arm rather than jumping from the shoulder to the elbow. Make use of the subtle sense of touch to smooth the path of the prāṇas through the tissues between each set of points.

Proceed through the points at a rate that ensures continuity of focus. As the practice deepens over time, there may be the appearance of points of light at each point of focus. There might also be a sense of actually being led through the practice rather than consciously directing the practice. One might also begin to identify and image the internal anatomy within oneself.

The accompanying table and diagram on the following two pages enumerate the points as they are to be followed. This may not be the only sequence of points for this practice, but it was the sequence originally taught to me.

Following the practice of 61 points, proceed to the practice of śīthalī karaṇa as described in step 3.

With practice and increased familiarity with yoga nidrā, some will skip steps 2 through 4, and proceed to step 5a. Please keep in mind that the body still needs to rest for several hours, even if consciousness is maintained during that deep rest.

***Something to consider:***

While learning lengthy practices, I would often wonder how to shorten the time needed to master the practice. How long have we been gifted to master our self-development? One life? More than just a lifetime? Compared to eternity, the time taken to master a practice, or any skill for that matter, seems relatively short.

# 61 Points

| Pt. | Focus | 31 | Heart Center |
|---|---|---|---|
| 1 | Between Eyebrows | 32 | Navel Center |
| 2 | Throat Center | 33 | Pelvic Region |
| 3 | Right Shoulder | 34 | Right Hip |
| 4 | Right Elbow | 35 | Right Knee |
| 5 | Right Wrist | 36 | Right Ankle |
| 6 | Tip of Right Thumb | 37 | Tip Right Big Toe |
| 7 | Tip Right Index F. | 38 | Tip Right 2nd Toe |
| 8 | Tip Right Middle F. | 39 | Tip Right 3rd Toe |
| 9 | Tip Right Ring F. | 40 | Tip Right 4th Toe |
| 10 | Tip Right Little F. | 41 | Tip Right 5th Toe |
| 11 | Right Wrist | 42 | Right Ankle |
| 12 | Right Elbow | 43 | Right Knee |
| 13 | Right Shoulder | 44 | Right Hip |
| 14 | Throat Center | 45 | Pelvic Region |
| 15 | Left Shoulder | 46 | Left Hip |
| 16 | Left Elbow | 47 | Left Knee |
| 17 | Left Wrist | 48 | Left Ankle |
| 18 | Tip of Left Thumb | 49 | Tip Left Big Toe |
| 19 | Tip Left Index F. | 50 | Tip Left 2nd Toe |
| 20 | Tip Left Middle F. | 51 | Tip Left 3rd Toe |
| 21 | Tip Left Ring F. | 52 | Tip Left 4th Toe |
| 22 | Tip Left Little F. | 53 | Tip Left 5th Toe |
| 23 | Left Wrist | 54 | Left Ankle |
| 24 | Left Elbow | 55 | Left Knee |
| 25 | Left Shoulder | 56 | Left Hip |
| 26 | Throat Center | 57 | Pelvic Region |
| 27 | Heart Center | 58 | Navel Center |
| 28 | Right Breast | 59 | Heart Center |
| 29 | Heart Center | 60 | Throat Center |
| 30 | Left Breast | 61 | Between Eyebrows |

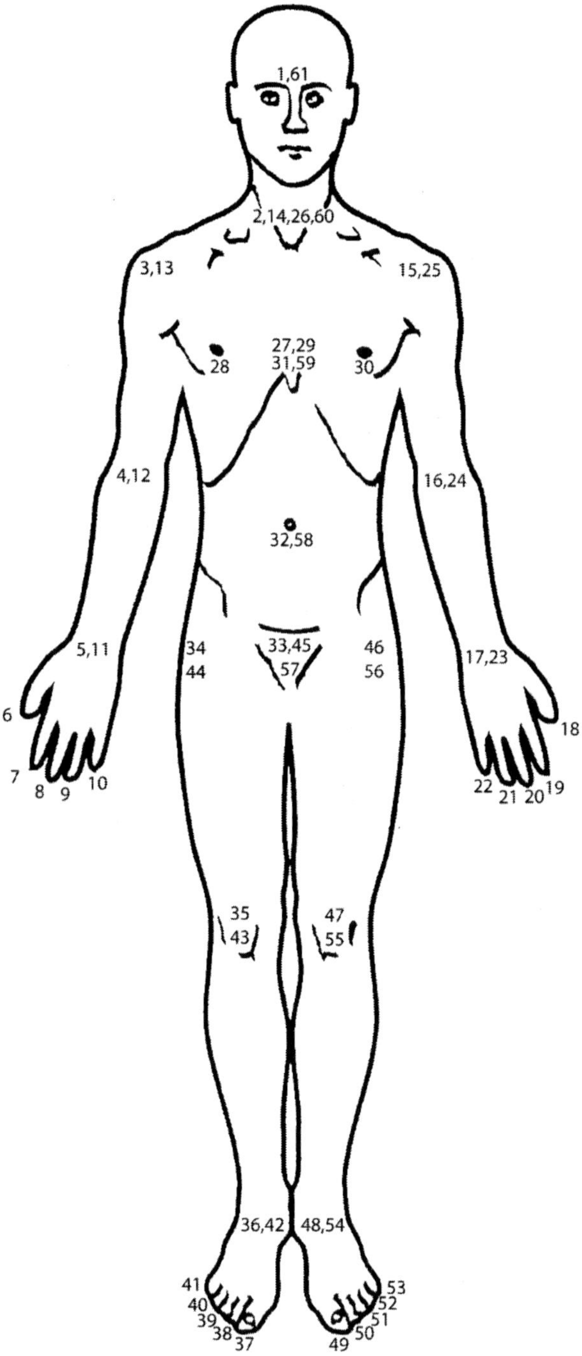
1,61
2,14,26,60
3,13
15,25
27,29
31,59
28
30
4,12
16,24
32,58
5,11
34
44
33,45
57
46
56
17,23
6
7
8
9
10
18
22
21
20
19
35
43
47
55
36,42
48,54
41
40
39
38
37
53
52
51
50
49

3. Śīthalī karaṇa is a practice to clear the prāṇa flow and the central channel between the cakras described in the previous chapter. This step was taught during the original presentation of yoga nidrā practice by my teacher. If one has been practicing the clearing methods for the central channel, śīthalī karaṇa and aum kriya, one may choose to simply survey the channel for any restrictions in flow and proceed with steps 4 through 8.

4. Lie on the left side and exhale and inhale ten times while focusing on the flow in the right nostril. Alternatively, one can breathe as if the entire right side of the body is flowing with prāṇa.

5. Lie on the right side and exhale and inhale ten times while focusing on the flow in the left nostril. Alternatively, one can breathe as if the entire left side of the body is flowing with prāṇa. The object of steps four and five is to get the nostrils to flow evenly if they are not already doing so.

5a. Variation to steps 4 and 5: Alternatively, one can remain supine and turn one's head to the side of the dominant nostril until the shift in dominance just begins to occur. If one has been training the nostrils as in the previous practices in this book, they will be more responsive to balancing.

6. Lie on the back and begin exhaling and inhaling with the whole body. On the exhale apāṇa moves down the central channel and out laterally at each cakra and outward through every pore of the body. On the inhale the prāṇa

moves inward laterally through every pore and cakra and then upward within the outer layer of the central channel.

7. Take three serene diaphragmatic breaths, merging the prāṇas and breath with the vibration of the mantra "soḥaṃ" at ājñā cakra.

8. By this time the central channel downward should be clearly in the mind's view. Bring the mind's focus to viśuddha cakra, and finally to anāhata cakra. Extend the exhalation to be longer than the inhalation until roughly a 2:1 ratio is reached. Keep the mind's focus within anāhata cakra. If iḍā and piṅgalā have been well balanced, the path downward beginning at the indentation above the upper lip should invite one to proceed downward through the center point of the chin, downward through the central area of viśuddha cakra, and behind the sternum to the central radiance of anāhata cakra.

While yoga nidrā can be an enhanced state of conscious awareness, it may also lead to other aspects of one's subtle anatomy, such as the cave of the heart, or access to Śri Cakra.

## Kevala Kumbhaka

One of the statements made by my teacher is that "The first thing students in the cave are taught is how to die." I have come to understand that he was referring to the state of kevala kumbhaka, where the prāṇas are regulated in a way that suspends for a time the need to breath with normal rates of respiration. As one gains more experience with the subtle self, the breath may be drawn to spontaneously suspend the need to breath. This can lead to a state of kevala kumbhaka that is very similar to a near death experience. While it is best to be initiated into the practice directly by one's teacher who is experienced in the practice, there are those students who come upon this state spontaneously and can benefit from knowing what is occurring.

Leading up to this state are some changes in focus accompanying changes in the breath:

**1.** Perfectly executed serene diaphragmatic breath is established. Not the slightest irregularity is present. The mind will be invited to silence.

**2.** Following this, there is an invitation to extend the diaphragmatic breath into a complete breath as the ribcage also begins to expand with the inhalation accompanying the abdominal expansion from the diaphragmatic breath. If one has been practicing ujjayi breath regularly, the chest expansion will also be perfectly smooth.

**3.** As the complete breath continues to expand, there is an invitation to attend to an area of absolute stillness called kūrma nādī just posterior to the upper sternum below the jugular notch. Accompanying this invitation is a developing bliss that becomes the focus of awareness.

**4.** The breath may then choose not to exhale or not to continue breathing. Surrendering to that invitation as well as not resisting the desire to breathe when it occurs may occur several times. One does not seek to control as in retention, but rather learns to surrender to the choice of the breath not to breathe. If iḍā and piṅgalā are perfectly balanced as one surrenders to the invitation to suspend the breath, one experiences pratyāhāra as one enters kevala kumbhaka, where breathing is suspended for a significant period of time.

**5.** As in a near death experience, a source of energy comes into awareness that sustains one for as long as one needs. This can appear as a point or area of brilliance from a particular cakra. There is also a nearly imperceptible exchange of air as the airways are still open and the heart may continue to beat. The quote of my teacher at the beginning of this book will reveal its truth.

"Guru is not a person. It is a force driven by grace."

Swami Rama

***Something to Consider:*** That force driven by grace called guru can take many forms, depending upon one's training, philosophy, and culture.

## Integration and Final Thoughts

As one progresses along the path of samāyā tantra, many unique, unexpected, and blissful experiences can manifest. My teacher emphasized that the experiences of one's practice are to be received without attachment. Seeking to repeat a revelation, color or other image, or any particular content of mind or ability can prevent progress. Acceptance of what is offered as a result of one's practice without desire or attachment is part of the mastery of yoga. Seeking the repetition of an experience can hinder progress on the path of discovery.

My teacher also emphasized that no matter the depth of one's yoga life, one should maintain the ability to focus on the daily tasks of life and be able to integrate with the everyday world. Retreating for a time to renew or to study and learn with more attention to one's yoga practice can be helpful. One is not ready to renounce the responsibilities of life and retreat to a cave, however, until one is able to fulfill the responsibilities of one's path in life from that cave. My teacher also said that if it were not for sages in the caves doing their work, the rain would not fall, and the rivers would not flow on this Earth.

# Sanskrit Pronunciation Guide

| | | | |
|---|---|---|---|
| a | h**u**m | m | **m**an or **m**utt |
| ā | f**a**ther | ṃ | o**m** (tongue raised) |
| ai | **ai**sle | n | **n**ap **n**ano **n**o |
| au | l**ou**d or cl**ou**d | ṅ | di**ng** or si**ng** |
| b | **b**ake | ṇ | k**n**ot or **n**ot |
| bh | a**bh**or | ñ | pi**ny**ata or ba**ny**an |
| c | **ch**at | o | n**o** or **o**pus |
| ch | Chur**ch h**ill | p | **p**utt or **p**ut |
| d | a**d** | ph | u**ph**ill |
| ḍ | **d**uh or **d**ull | r | **r**um or **r**oot |
| dh | a**dh**ere | ṛ | w**ri**t |
| ḍh | Bu**ddh**a or si**ddh**i | ṝ | whi**rr**ing |
| e | s**a**y or pr**a**y | s | **s**at, **s**un or **so**lve |
| g | **g**o | ś | **sh**ock or **sh**awl |
| gh | **gh**ee | ṣ | pu**sh** or hu**sh** |
| ḥ | **h**armony or **h**arm | t | **tat** or wa**t**er |
| h | **h**at | ṭ | **t**ime or **t**as**t**e |
| i | **i**t or h**i**t | th | an**th**ill |
| ī | s**ee**n or pol**i**ce | ṭh | **Th**ailand ligh**th**ouse |
| j | **j**abber or **j**ut | u | p**u**sh or b**u**llet |
| jh | jud**ge h**er hed**geh**og | | |
| k | **c**amera or **c**ar | ū | r**u**de or sp**oo**n |
| kh | an**kh** | v | **v**odka; vibrating w |
| l | **l**amp or **l**amb | y | **y**ap or **y**es |
| ḷ | cava**l**ry or reve**l**ry | | |

The Sanskrit alphabet has an order that differs alphabetically from the above pronunciation table.

# Glossary

This is an expanded glossary that also contains terms used in Practical Yoga Sūtras by this author as well as many yoga writings.

| | |
|---|---|
| **abhiniveśa** | desire for life sustained by its own potency |
| **abhyāsa** | practice, as in sustained effort |
| **agnisāra** | essence of fire element |
| **ahaṃkāra** | ego; sense of individual I-am-ness |
| **ahiṃsā** | non-harming; non-violence |
| **ājñā cakra** | so-called third eye center where iḍā, piṅgalā, and suṣumnā intersect |
| **ākāśa** | ether or space |
| **ākuñcana** | contraction |
| **āliṅga** | as yet without differentiation or characteristics |
| **anāhata cakra** | heart center |
| **aparigraha** | non-aquisitiveness |
| **asaṃprajñāta** | A state of total insight not requiring supportive factors such as an object of focus |
| **āsanas** | yoga poses |

| | |
|---|---|
| **asmitā** | Blending together of the power of pure consciousness with the power of cognition; the one who apprehends |
| **asteya** | non-stealing |
| **ātman** | divine spark that is part of an individual soul |
| **avidyā** | lack of knowledge |
| **aviśeṣa** | universal or non-specific |
| **bāhya kumbhaka** | retention after exhale; holding outside the vessel |
| **bhāvanā** | dwelling upon in the mind, cultivating and absorbing a meaning |
| **bhūtas** | elements; earth, water, fire, air, ether or space |
| **bīja** | Seed |
| **brahmacarya** | walking the path of Brahman |
| **buddhi** | discriminative faculty of the mind |
| **citta-vṛitti** | storehouse of impressions of the mind |

| | |
|---|---|
| **citta-vṛitti-nirodha** | silence of the waves of the mind |
| **dhāranā** | concentration; focus |
| **dharma** | condition or property; attribute |
| **dharmī** | property holder, the nature or that which is the thing in past, present, and future forms |
| **dhyāna** | the state of meditation |
| **dveṣaḥ** | Repulsion accompanying pain |
| **ekāgratā** | one-pointedness of mind |
| **ekāgratā pariṅāma** | one-pointedness on a temporary state of mind |
| **guṇas** | tendencies that are part of the process of manifestation |
| **Haṃsa** | That I am; swan as a symbol of the source of oneself |
| **hatha** | solar-lunar; right-left |
| **iḍā** | left or lunar energy channel |
| **Iśvara** | that divine consciousness untouched by the afflictions of life |

| | |
|---|---|
| **Iśvara-praṇidhāna** | Iśvara, the Divine; praṇidhāna, practicing in the presence of; surrendering to the presence of the Divine or self-surrendering to Self |
| **japa** | systematic mental repetition of a mantra |
| **Kaivalya** | Self-realization; liberated; isolation of the self from all matter |
| **karaṇa** | taking up a matter in question or an activity, such as a dance routine or a routine of a specific yoga practice. |
| **karmas** | actions (thought, words spoken, deeds) and their repercussions |
| **kevala kumbhaka** | suspension of need to breath |
| **kirtan** | call and response devotional chanting intended to open the heart of participants to the Divine |
| **kleśas** | painful pollutants of the mind |
| **kośa** | sheath |
| **kriya** | preliminary or preparatory |
| **kumbhaka** | retention of breath |

| | |
|---|---|
| **kuṇḍalinī** | force of manifestation, feminine aspect of the Divine, first prāṇa |
| **kūrma nādī** | tortoise tube |
| **liṅga – mātra** | identifier, such as fruit as an identifier for both an orange and an apple |
| **maṇḍala** | circle; art form for spiritual or ritual art |
| **mantra** | sound, series of sounds or phrases used in yoga practices |
| **māyā** | erroneous self- identification of being an individual; the manifest universe and the Śakti that participates in its creation |
| **mudra** | gesture |
| **maṇipūra cakra** | navel center |
| **mūlādhāra cakra** | root center |
| **nādī** | subtle energy channel or pathway |

| | |
|---|---|
| **nādī ṣodhana** | purification of the nervous system; alternate nostril breathing; purification of the nādīs |
| **nidrā** | sleep; of sleep |
| **nirbīja** | without seed |
| **niyamas** | observances; austerities for conducting life |
| **pāda** | foot, or footprint, one of four sections or parts |
| **pariṅāma** | temporary state of mind |
| **piṅgalā** | right or solar energy channel |
| **Prakṛiti** | universal nature, the manifest |
| **prāṇa** | subtle energy of any physical object or mental impression |
| **prāṇayāma** | regulation of the subtle energies |
| **prasāraṇa** | expansion |
| **pratyāhāra** | withdrawal of the gross senses |
| **pratyaya** | seed or content of the mind at a given moment |
| **Puruṣa** | the potential for all, not yet manifest |

| | |
|---|---|
| **rāgaḥ** | attraction that accompanies pleasure |
| **sabīja** | with seed |
| **sādhanā** | means of accomplishing something; discipline or practice |
| **sahasrāra cakra** | crown center |
| **Śakti** | Divine Mother; feminine force of manifestation |
| **śaktipāta** | an act of grace where the Divine energy serves to illuminate one in some way |
| **samādhi** | expanded state of conscious awareness |
| **saṃprajñāta** | total insight requiring supportive factors such as an object of focus |
| **saṃskāra** | impression in the mind |
| **saṃtoṣa** | Contentment |
| **saṃyama** | simultaneous application of dhāranā, dhyāna, and samādhi |

| | |
|---|---|
| **sānanda** | sa, with or accompanied by, ānanda, rapture or bliss |
| **sasmitā** | sa, with or accompanied by, asmitā, I-am-ness |
| **satya** | truthfulness |
| **śauca** | Purity |
| **śavāsana** | corpse pose |
| **siddhis** | attainments resulting from yoga practice |
| **śīthalī karaṇa** | progressively ascending breath |
| **Śiva** | divine potential; male aspect of the Divine |
| **smṛti** | Mindfulness |
| **soḥaṃ** | I am That; derivative of Haṃsa mantra |
| **sūrya vidyā** | solar science |
| **suṣumnā** | central energy pathway |
| **sūtra** | thread; concise phrase or presentation |

| | |
|---|---|
| **Svādhyāya** | Self-study leading to purification; study of one's own lesson |
| **svādiṣṭhāna cakra** | sacral center |
| **tapas** | self-discipline; austerity |
| **trikoṇāsana** | triangle pose |
| **vairāgya** | cessation of desires |
| **vāsanā** | subconscious impression |
| **vibhūti** | powerful expansions; sacred ash, results of preparation through yoga disciplines |
| **vicāra** | refined or subtle thought |
| **vipāka** | fruits of one's actions |
| **viśeṣa** | particular or specific |
| **viśuddha cakra** | throat center |
| **vitarka** | thought accompanied by names of particular objects of focus; gross thought |
| **vivek - khyātiḥ** | knowledge of discrimination of the real from the unreal |

| | |
|---|---|
| **vṛitti** | modification of the mind; impression in the mind; wave of the mind; operation of the mind |
| **yamas** | attitudes with which to conduct one's life |
| **yantra** | three-dimensional form of a maṇḍala; a vibration or admixture of vibrations that assumes a three-dimensional form |
| **yoga** | union; bind together or yoke |